William McInnes is one of Australia's most popular stage and screen actors. His leading roles in *SeaChange* and *Blue Heelers* have made him a household name. The mini-series *Shark Net* and *My Brother Jack* earned him widespread critical acclaim. He has been nominated for numerous stage and screen awards, and has won a Variety Club Drama Award in 1997 and two Logie awards for Most Outstanding Actor in 2000 and 2004.

William grew up in Queensland and has travelled extensively throughout Australia. He now lives in Melbourne with his wife, the film-maker Sarah Watt, and their two children. *A Man's Got to Have a Hobby* is his first book. William's novel, *Cricket Kings*, is about a neighbourhood cricket team, the Yarraville West Fourths.

Also by William McInnes
Cricket Kings

William McInnes

A man's got to have a hobby

Long summers with my dad

HACHETTE AUSTRALIA

'Love is the Sweetest Thing'—Ray Noble © 1932 Francis Day and Hunter Ltd.
For Australia and New Zealand: J. Albert & Son Pty Limited
International copyright secured. All rights reserved. Used by permission

HACHETTE AUSTRALIA

First published in Australia and New Zealand in 2005
by Hodder Australia
(An imprint of Hachette Livre Australia Pty Limited)
Level 17, 207 Kent Street, Sydney NSW 2000
Website: www.hachette.com.au

Reprinted 2005 (four times)

This edition published in 2006
Reprinted 2006, 2007 (twice), 2008

Copyright © William McInnes 2005

National Library of Australia
Cataloguing-in-Publication data

McInnes, William.
  A man's got to have a hobby : long summers with my Dad.

  ISBN 978 0 7336 2078 2.

  1. McInnes, William - Childhood and youth. 2. Actors -
  Queensland - Biography. 3. Fathers and sons - Queensland -
  Biography. Title.

792.028092

Text design and typesetting by Bookhouse, Sydney
Cover design by Christabella Designs
Family photos from McInnes family collection
Author photo by Rebecca Thornton
Printed in Australia by Griffin Press, Adelaide

Hachette Livre Australia's policy is to use papers that are natural, renewable and recyclable products
and made from wood grown in sustainable forests. The logging and manufacturing processes are
expected to conform to the environmental regulations of the country of origin.

This book is dedicated to Dad and Mum,
Vaughan, Laurie, Rhian, Corby and Aunty Rita.

A Fine Vessel

1

I am sitting in the study of my mum's house in Redcliffe. I'm trying to use the phone. To be precise I'm actually trying to find a telephone number so I can use the phone. Trying to find the number and then trying to find the phone could be a protracted exercise – the study in the house I grew up in can derail the most determined efforts at efficient purpose. For as long as I can remember the phone has been here in the study, although finding the thing was never easy, even when it was that great, heavy-set, black blob of Bakelite with an arm-breaking handpiece. Nowadays, the thin white plastic number could be anywhere.

A certain state of flux exists in this house, and the study is a case in point. The study wasn't always the study; it was once called 'the Den'. It was my father's den. What my father did in his den I was never quite sure. He would come home and throw things in through the internal door of his den and then prowl off. 'Don't touch *anything* in the den,' we'd be warned. Later, when my old man started his mostly handmade hire business, the 'Den' became the 'Office'. By this stage the office had two doors into it, the internal door and another rather grand door that faced out onto the front lawn. This door had a sign on it. A sign that said 'Office' on a door that never opened. People would come around to hire something and, quite naturally, they would walk to the door marked 'Office'. They had no idea it didn't open.

My father did. He could never understand why others wouldn't know this fact, so every time it happened he'd become more and more exasperated and cranky. He'd rush from the front door of the house, which *did* open, yelling, 'No, no, no, for Christ's sake. The bloody door doesn't open.'

Those who knew Dad well sometimes tried to open the office door for a laugh. But a lot of the newer customers were quite shocked. One day an old painter in his overalls shrieked as he fell back over a lump of concrete in the vague shape of a garden gnome. We thought he'd had a heart attack.

It was odd because it was Cliffy Jenkins. He was one of Dad's regulars and was having his little joke. But, unknown to Cliffy, Dad had decided to add yet another door so that he could come around behind the office.

Dad bent over his elderly friend. 'Cliffy, Cliffy?' he said. My sister Corby suggested he resuscitate him. Dad had been having breakfast – his morning fry-up of immense proportions – and his lips were slathered in oil and sauce. Cliffy's eyes opened and saw my father looming and puckering above him. He shrieked again. He was helped up, moaning. 'You and your bloody house, you've changed it again!'

My father looked down at his friend and patted him on his shoulder. 'Well, Cliffy,' he said. 'A man's got to have a hobby.'

That was the thing about this house; like life it was always changing. Walls would disappear overnight to reappear somewhere else the next day. A door that led into a pantry in the morning would open up onto a courtyard in the afternoon.

Anyway, I'm sitting in this study trying to use the phone, trying to find a phone number. I reach for a small box of telephone cards. The box was a present Mum received a couple of years ago. I open it and go to the list of cards in alphabetical order. Where the card marked 'L to P' should be is a card of similar size. It's not a telephone card. It is in fact a card from a Nabisco breakfast cereal called Granox. It is a collector's card – 'Our Modern Australia'. It has an illustration of a man in a slouch hat, walking at the head of a column of 'fuzzy wuzzies'. The card is entitled 'Walkabout in Our Savage Colony New Guinea'. It's forty years old, almost as old as me, and it's in a telephone box that's only two Christmases old.

I don't know how it got there, but it doesn't surprise me. This house has a mind of its own. In fact, it has so embedded itself in *my* heart and mind that I barely think of it as a house. My children refer to it simply as Nanna Mac's. They speak of it as you would a living thing. That is the key, my children see this house by a fire station as a living thing. Over the years it's soaked up the sounds and life around it like a sponge

5

soaks up the water in a bucket. But instead of squeezing the sponge dry and letting the water fall and trickle away, the house has retained it all. It holds on to memories that were thought long forgotten.

Perhaps that is why it looks bigger than it is. It's a two-storey rambling weatherboard with wraparound verandahs and a cluttered green yard. It's set back from a main road, down a quiet lane. It rests on a battleaxe block. Behind the fire station and the car park of a Senior Citizens' Hall. Before the Senior Cits' Hall was built there was a small, two-bedroom house on a large, deep allotment. That's where Mr Tibby lived.

Mr Tibby always looked to me like the man in the big Pilsener billboard by the trotting track. Bald-headed, pale-eyed and pink-faced, asking all that looked up, 'Won't you join me in a Pilsener?' The man in the billboard offered a foamy substance in a glass.

Mr Tibby was a widower. A big bull of a man, he walked with a thick stick, propping himself on it from time to time to heave at his wide belt and pull his trousers up over his huge stomach. He was a Jehovah's Witness. Once a week he'd come to the front door as we ate dinner. He'd lean on his stick and read us passages from the Bible. You could always tell he was coming by the thudding of his cane. He'd ask my mother how the children would get to heaven. 'Wrap them up in sacks would be best,' he'd say. He was constantly throwing sacks over the fence.

'Thank you very much,' my mother would say. 'Very kind. What a handy sack.' Then she'd look back and shake her head.

Whenever there was a full moon, Mr Tibby would walk up and down his deep block of land in his baggy underwear roaring quotes from the Bible. We children always felt safe in the house, even when Dad had to go to hospital with a bad foot. But Mum wasn't so soothed. She slept with a great wood axe under her pillow. When I'd go into my parents' room for an extra cuddle, I'd feel the blade. 'Just in case of Mr Tibby and his sacks,' Mum would say. I'd go back to my bed and the creaking timbers would reassure me. The breathing house made me safe.

Mr Tibby would sometimes ask us if we wanted to pick strawberries in his paddock. He would point them out with his great stick. I thought this big rumbling man would break my fingers as he thrust his heavy lump of wood here and there at the strawberries, smashing them even when it was clear our young eyes couldn't see them. 'Are ya blind? Are ya blind?' he'd cry.

Often he'd wait outside his house, dressed in his best, waiting for other Jehovah's Witnesses to come and take him to church. But they never did. One day he wasn't there any more. Dad said they'd put him away. His house stood empty. When, some time later, Mum told me he'd died I didn't feel anything much. I just thought of him smashing the strawberries into a bloody pulp.

His children sold his house and one afternoon when I came home from school, it was gone. Razed to the ground.

•

At eight o'clock every morning the fire signal would ring. This was the fire drill at the station. It was a sound that didn't startle as it began as a slow humming and would build to a soaring roar, not unlike a huge early-morning yawn. The firemen would saunter about laughing and singing; all men, away from their wives and families, carrying on like real lads. Flirting with Mum and my sisters. Harmless stuff. Jonsey with his battered face and smiling eyes, offering Mum freshly caught crabs and whiting from Woody Point Pier. Cherokee, who was from New Zealand, was given the moniker because he'd whoop like an Indian from a Western movie when he jumped aboard the fire engine. He'd sing songs that would echo off the big incinerator at the bottom of the station while Mum would be chopping wood in our backyard. I'd sit by the chopping block and hear him. 'Cheryl Moana Marie', he'd croon. It was an old John Rawls lounge number about a lonely man pining for his Maori princess.

One morning I heard a sharp, harsh breathing sound coming from the backyard. There was a knock at the door and there was Jonsey wearing his breathing apparatus and holding a bucket of sand crabs. Through his mask I could see his laughing eyes. He'd whistle while he walked around the grounds. High and clear. He would wear his cap at an angle and would never have a cigarette too far from his mouth. Sometimes he'd call me over to see if I could kick or pass a footy into a big white bucket he'd be holding.

'Come on, young Mac, come on over. Give it a drill and see how you go!' When the ball landed in the bucket he'd whistle his high sweet whistle. 'Never seen a ball fly like that, young Mac. Never.' And then he'd smile.

One Saturday night we heard the siren wail and the firemen shouting and the fire engines roaring to life. We all went and stood on the front verandah and could see a fire in a house down towards the beach. The first fire truck roared off with Cherokee howling; moments later the second engine began growling from the station. As it picked up speed and began to rocket down the road, a uniformed figure with blond hair sprinted after it holding his helmet in one hand.

'Hey, look at him go!' my brother yelled.

'He won't make it!' said one of my sisters.

But then just as the truck seemed to draw away, the uniformed figure flung himself at full stretch through the air and grabbed onto the rails on the back. The truck fishtailed and tyre smoke billowed as it braked sharply.

'He's the flying Dutchman,' said Mum.

'He's the flying Dutchman, all right,' said Dad.

From then on the young, raw-boned blond man with the Dutch name became the Flying Dutchman.

One of the brigade officers, Mr Easton, would sometimes walk his trotter around the station's back paddock. Jonsey would whistle a starting tune and do a phantom racecall. Mr Easton's horse always looked a certain winner and sure enough he'd never fail to lose. Both of them would laugh and I would join in.

Mr Easton had a son who was allowed to keep pigeons up the back of the station. In those days he was called spastic –

now you'd say he had cerebral palsy. It was hard to understand him when he spoke and when he'd try to speak louder, he would often spit and dribble. This he usually did at his swine of a dog, Karl. Karl was a psychotic German shepherd that we'd race through the station, if we felt brave or bored enough.

'Goin' out to race Karl,' one of us kids would say for no particular reason. And then it was on.

'Betcha you don't make it to the bomb shelter.'

'Betcha I can.'

'Betcha you can't.'

'Betcha a packet of Beachies I can.'

'No short cuts!'

I was the youngest by six years and was easy prey for Karl. I seldom made it past the 'bomb shelter', a round brick building built in the 1950s. So I'd invariably lose lots of Beachies, a type of pelleted chewing gum we'd buy from the service station up on the corner.

Sometimes I wouldn't even make it to the bomb shelter – I'd only get as far as the tennis courts. One morning I screamed and leapt up at the sharp wire netting that bound the courts. The metal stuck into my fingers and toes, while below me Karl leapt and snarled, and Mr Easton's son bellowed and dribbled. On the court a doubles game was in full swing.

'I just don't like a man who marries a woman who is *sooo* much younger than he is,' said a big woman in a small hat and a ballooning tennis skirt. 'But I could never vote for that Whitlam fellow…' She finished off her thought as I clung onto the wire, 'He may not be a communist but I'm *sure* he's a socialist.' She stopped and turned to look at me. She was wearing green-black clip-on shades attached to the top of her glasses and I could see the whole scene reflected in her specs – me and Karl and Mr Easton's son, who had a hold of the dog's collar and was being shaken like a go-go dancer.

And way behind us I could see our house. I hung there in her sunglasses for what seemed like ages. Karl was eventually dragged off by the gurgling Easton boy and I jumped down and ran off along the fence. I heard the big woman as I ran. 'A *socialist*,' she snapped, and then she hit the tennis ball.

Occasionally we'd play on the courts with old wooden racquets named after Aussie champions who were on the pension even then. Men like Frank Sedgman and Fred Stolle. I was given a Pancho Gonzales Special. What was so special about the racquet was lost on me, although it did have a pleasant image of Pancho smiling rakishly from the neck of the racquet and the head was bent at what could only be called an alarming angle.

The tennis courts were made of light crushed rock and sand so if you played barefoot, pebbles and bits and pieces would stick into your feet. You could slide, though, and it wasn't long before gouging big skids into the sand became the object of the whole exercise.

During one game I moaned incessantly in my youngest-child whine. 'I can't play because my Pancho Gonzales is bent!'

'A bad tradesman always blames his tools,' my mother said.

'It's bent, it's bent, Mum!'

'If you don't want to play, you don't have to play.'

'It's bent, it's bent, it's no good!'

'What's he whingeing about now?' My father sauntered over. He never played tennis and he never came near the court, so it was a bit of a surprise to see him. He'd been working, making deliveries or pulling down walls, or whatever and he was dressed as if he'd been up to something. He loved hats, 'dynamic' hats, he'd call them, which really meant 'work' hats. He preferred peaked caps, especially Makita caps, which were the red and orange ones supplied by the Japanese power tool company. But today he had on what he called his 'Robin Hood number' – a strange, chequered, bucket-shaped thing that he'd mangled into something vaguely resembling the hat worn by one of Robin Hood's merry men from the television show. He was also wearing his brown Stubbies work shorts, a white T-shirt, footy socks and work boots.

He ambled through the gates of the court.

'Pancho bloody Gonzales was a legend, son, he'd eat people alive,' he said.

'But the racquet's *bent*, it's no good.'

'If Pancho put his name to it then it's all right. Just play the game.'

'It's not his racquet, Dad, it came from a jumble sale.'

My father looked at me. 'Oh, all right,' he said, nodding his head, 'not good enough for you, eh?'

'Oh, Colin,' my mother sighed.

'No, it's all right, love. Give me that thing, you.' He grabbed Pancho's racquet and told my sister to give me hers – a Phil

Dent Special that had been bought from Woolies down the road for her birthday. It was a prehistoric aluminium number but back then I guess it was pretty space-age.

My sisters started to giggle.

My mother looked at my father, wide-eyed. 'You're not going to play, are you?'

'It's all right, I know what I'm about. Come on, you goose, me and Pancho'll knock you into next week.' Dad flipped the racquet and looked at it for the first time. He ran his fingers around its bent head. 'Christ,' he mumbled.

I lobbed the ball to him and the show began. He swung the racquet like he was felling a tree, and the ball shot off at crazy angles again and again. He waved his arms about so much that his dynamic Robin Hood hat flopped in front of his eyes and his big chook legs skated and skidded across the court, his feet scrabbling in his work boots.

'This bloody game's for penguins. Bloody Pancho Gonzales.' He held the racquet aloft. 'It's as bent as an S-bend. You could scratch someone's arse around the corner.'

'Colin!' my mother said.

'Well!' he answered with a laugh.

We heard more laughter and turned to see that Jonsey and the Flying Dutchman had wandered over and were standing there shaking their heads.

'How'd you be, brother?' Dad said to Jonsey.

Jonsey looked back at my father. 'I didn't know you played tennis.'

My father stared a minute and then casually flipped his bent Pancho Gonzales Special, caught it and pushed back his Robin Hood number. 'Well, Jonsey,' he said. 'A man's got to have a hobby.'

2

Our house on the battleaxe block was bounded by trees, and birds would gather in the branches as the fruit ripened, clattering and eating, carrying on and dropping berries onto the tin roof. This particular sound – a kind of music really – would mix with the other peculiar sounds of my family. Mum and Dad singing and yelling. Mum calling for the dog. Dad banging away on the next renovation. My sisters shrieking with laughter in the backyard as they gave each other different hairstyles and colour jobs. My brother hacking away on the piano that has never been in tune, in all the time it has been sitting downstairs against the wall.

Music filled the house, and surrounded it. From over the backyard fence would come the noise of our neighbours, the Worths, and their record player. Reg and Warren, sons of Snow and Pat Worth, loved Johnny Cash and Johnny O'Keefe. And Engelbert Humperdinck. And they especially loved the races. So the music was often accompanied by a jaunty racing trumpet and the flat nasal excitement of the caller.

Every now and then lyrics of the songs would float across those yards, adding a backdrop to the domestic action of the day. It was a cacophony of life. Of living.

I remember sitting drinking sarsaparilla in the backyard while watching my mother chop wood to the tune of 'Spanish Flea', an insane Tijuana trumpet song. Then later watching Dad stretched out on a trestle table having a midday 'kip' while Mario Lanza wailed from the hi-fi next door. Just as Mario reached his high-pitched crescendo he paused to gather breath but before he could assault our ears again my dozing father let rip an almighty fart. 'Merry Christmas to you too, you fat bastard,' he muttered, spreadeagled on his trestle table.

One beautiful, still summer's day only one song played. It was late summer for the mangoes had started to ripen and fall. In those last moments of the afternoon, when the heat was at its strongest and the humidity had started to close in, before the thunderstorm rolled across the bay, I lay on the deep green couch grass and stared up at the sky. Our dog Sam was next to me panting, and from downstairs came the sound of my sister Laurie playing 'Claire De Lune' on the old piano. She played that piece over and over again. I lay there until the rain and the darkness came. I thought I had never heard anything as beautiful.

The backyard at the battleaxe block was a place where you could dream. It seemed huge when I was a boy and yet now when I stand there I see how close to the fence line the houses next door have crept and how many trees have been chopped down. But it doesn't take long before the big trees grow again, and the houses disappear, waiting for the memories to put everything into perspective. Life goes by so fast that sometimes it is good to wait and let the memories catch up. And there is no better place to do that than the backyard where you grew up.

We kept chooks that lived in the corner by the woodpile, and every morning while Mum walked about calling her 'chook-chook-chooky' song, flinging around last night's leftovers, I'd have to brave the flame-combed rooster to check for eggs. The chooks were good value, especially when little boys became Tarzan, stalking jungle beast and prey. Chooks doubled as all manner of big cats and elephants; but not the old flame-combed rooster – he had a habit of pecking the jungle king's toes and sending Tarzan tearfully into his mother's arms.

Around the side of the chook house is where I saved the world from disaster.

Beneath the spreading branches of our Moreton Bay fig was a place of darkness and mystery – the woodpile and the chopping block. Dad used to call it the 'Last Chook Stop'. I used to stand on the chopping block dancing and serenading the chooks – bastardised Dean Martin songs usually – unintentionally mocking their fate. I would wail, 'I love you and don't you forget it!' all the while picking feathers and blood from between my toes.

There was always the vague air of darkness in the woodpile. The air of strangeness and of otherworldliness.

It was here that my brother, while attempting to chop wood with the help of my sister, missed the block of wood entirely and cut off the top joint of one of her fingers. He acted quickly, offering her some money and a lolly not to tell Dad. She almost went along with his suggestion, but Mum was even quicker. She threw the bit of finger into Mr Tibby's paddock so our dog wouldn't get it. I can only guess at the doctor's reaction.

My father acted quicker still. At the time he was engaged in one of his unsuccessful attempts to gain election to state parliament, and somehow he managed to get a photo of my brother and smiling sister, complete with her hand swathed in huge bandages, into the local newspaper. The article spoke of my father's concerns for good parenting.

He didn't win that election either.

One of the backyard's great mysteries occurred in that woodpile. I had borrowed Malcolm Parish's GI Joe doll and stood on the last chook stop while throwing him up through the branches. I'd watch him hang for a moment while his plastic limbs seemed to float against the sky and then he'd tangle and plummet back to me. I'd do this over and over. Up he went for the tenth time and…he never came back. Lost, swallowed by the mystery of the woodpile. I never told Malcolm how GI Joe disappeared – I thought it better to say that he was taken by our dog. It was easier to say that than try to explain that the woodpile was not unlike the Bermuda Triangle.

Often I would climb up the biggest of the Moreton Bay figs and sit there among the birds. Sometimes I'd read books but mostly I'd just sit in the crook of a limb and dream and sing to myself.

From up there I could hear the Easton boy talking to his pigeons below. The birds would make soft sounds and he would coo and hum back to them. It was a lovely sound and I would lie back in the tree and listen and watch the sky and be happy.

The woodpile wasn't just a vortex for the unexplainable. It was where the men would gather. I'd lie in my bed at night and hear the cicadas call and the trees rustle and the low voices of my father and his friends. Rumbling laughter and the clinking of glass meant that the men were talking politics. Occasionally he'd hold more formal political gatherings down at the old Seabrae Hotel at the end of Anzac Avenue. By this stage my father was enthusiastically immersing himself in Labor politics. Fundraising events such as chook raffles were the major focus. Mysteriously, a gentleman who bore a keen resemblance to my father's mate Uncle Reg would win each time.

After I was born Dad calmed down slightly, but I can remember one gathering he held in our backyard. Corby and I sat under the wonky back steps as Mum came down in a voluminous floral dress carrying a tray of food. The men standing around our yard were scrubbed and cleaned and shining and smelled of Brylcreem, bad deodorant and tobacco. They were wearing oddly coloured acrylic safari pantsuits and they all sported sideburns. It was like the entire cast from some old Jungle Jim movie had wandered in. Only instead of being in black and white these loud big game hunters wore safari suits in the same colours as my textas. Pastels and limes and oranges. The men turned as one when they heard Mum's voice: 'Here they are, boys, devils on horseback!' Prunes wrapped in strands of bacon and skewered by a toothpick. The men ooooed and ahhhed, devouring the tiny canapes. One Jungle Jim even went so far as to bend his leg and pretend to fart in time to the music as the Tijuana Taxi honked its horn from the stereo.

'Who *are* they?' I whispered to Corby.

'They...' she said, before pausing, taking these strange beings in. 'They are the Labor Party.'

To this day I have trouble separating 'Tijuana Taxi' and pastel-coloured safari suits from the Labor Party.

In summer the backyard became the MCG, and in winter, Lang Park. Screaming and weaving with my Woolies plastic footy tucked under my arm, I led the Queensland team to successive heroic victories over the New South Wales Blues. My sisters and I would listen to the football calls on the radio and act out the game. I'd usually take over the commentary and screech the glorious play I was making. I'd fling my skinny frame this way and that, and try to send my sisters off when they tackled too hard. My father would watch with mild interest but if I went on too long he'd mutter, 'Get a grip son, rein it in.' When my exertions grew more enthusiastic and my rantings became less decipherable, he'd stare at me with a furrowed brow before turning to Mum and asking, 'What's wrong with your son?'

But it was in summer that the backyard really came into its own. Dad had built a barbecue that resembled an air-raid shelter crossed with some sort of bizarre pagan temple. Whenever we fired it up, it'd belch smoke like the German battleship the *Bismarck* on full attack. People would disappear behind a black wall of smoke with a slice of bread in their hand and reappear minutes later disorientated, with streaming eyes and a hacking cough. If they were lucky while they were 'missing' they might also score a half-cooked piece of meat.

I have a vivid memory of my father tying a hanky around his face, pulling his Makita cap down over his eyes, then nodding to Mum like Humphrey Bogart did to Ingrid Bergman in *Casablanca* before surging off into the black wall to cook. All you could hear was, 'Jesus bloody Christ... I need bloody radar!'

Woe betide anyone who was choosy about what they got to eat. 'Listen, you piecan,' he'd say, 'you want a rissole, you go in there and get one. I'm strictly dealing in lucky dips today. Jesus bloody wept!'

We thought we'd lost Aunty Rita for good one barbecue when she offered to cook. We eventually found her down behind the banana trees. Mum rushed back for a glass of Scotch, saying that Aunty Rita looked like 'a bloody black and white minstrel'.

Perhaps it wasn't the best barbecue for cooking, but throw a golf ball against it and you had the West Indies' fast bowlers as well as Lillee and Thomson right there in the backyard.

Unfortunately I ended up playing the golf ball a lot more with my head than with my bat, and the measured tones of the cricket commentator would be replaced with howling and tears as a huge egg appeared on my noggin. This lead to an innovation in cricket: it's not generally acknowledged but it was me, William McInnes, at the tender age of eleven, who introduced protective headgear to the national game. In 1975 with Lillee and Thomson and the Windies at the height of their powers, I dared to experiment. At first I used my sister's motorbike helmet. Laurie had recently bought a Vespa scooter and I used her funny peaked scooter helmet to protect myself from golf balls richocheting off the barbecue. The problem was that this helmet wasn't a full-face job and although it worked okay for an over or two, the barbecue sorted me out when I copped one flush on the nose.

I put the helmet away and started on a design that I felt more comfortable with. I took Mum's red wash bucket and a pair of scissors, cut two eyeholes and then stabbed a few smaller holes for air. I then wrapped my head in a couple of beanies and a towel so the bucket was a nice tight fit. So effective was this headgear that I dispensed with the bat and would simply peg the golf ball against the barbecue and then head-bucket bunt it to all parts of the ground. Lillee and Thomson never knew what hit them.

All the while I commentated away merrily. 'There's no way through his defence.' *Thump.* 'That one hurt a little bit but it still raced away for four.' *Thump.* I stopped when I heard a muffled roar. Before I knew what was what I was wrenched around and I could see my father staring at me through the eyeholes.

'What the bloody hell do you think you're doing, you pillock?'

'Playing cricket!' I yelled.

'You what?' He looked stunned. His mouth was agape.

'Playing cricket!' I shouted again, very slowly this time. I sounded like a prepubescent Darth Vader.

'With a bucket on your head? You have a bucket on your head!' He seemed to be having trouble coming to terms with this new development in the game.

'It's my bucket helmet. It protects me from the golf ball... and the barbecue.' My father continued to stare at me. I decided to illustrate my connection to the game. 'Don Bradman used to play with a golf ball and a –'

'Don Bradman *never* played cricket with a bucket on his head.'

'He only played against a water tank not a barbecue.'

'Don bloody Bradman would have eaten that barbecue alive,' my father snorted. 'You are not Don Bradman.'

I took his point. 'That's why I need my bucket helmet.'

My father looked hard at me. He took a few deep breaths, made a few exclamations and a few false starts at yelling, but he began to see. 'That thing protects you, does it?'

I nodded my bucket in agreement.

'The golf ball doesn't hurt you?'

I shook my bucket.

My father thought for a moment. 'Give us that golf ball and stand over there.'

I couldn't really see where 'over there' was, but I guessed a direction and headed off.

A golf ball hit me.

'Did that hurt?' my father asked.

I shook my bucket again. 'No, Dad, it did not.'

'Well, I'll be buggered.'

Thereafter we spent a happy half an hour or so with my father throwing golf balls at my head. It was only stopped by my mother asking where her red wash bucket was. At that point Dad hurried off.

'Sorry, son, you're on your own with this one.'

Dad loved building things and, once constructed, whatever the object was, it would need an atom bomb to move it. Planning was never a big thing in Dad's vision, but flushed with the success of the *Bismarck* barbecue, he decided to build an incinerator.

An incinerator. The word rolls off the tongue.

The ritualistic burning off of household and garden rubbish is a thing of the past, but in those days the backyard incinerator was an icon of suburbia. Dad's incinerator was not so much a functioning device as a statement of his love for Mum. It was big and it burned and it was right next to the washing line. When Mum pointed this out my father stood back, aghast. He pointed to the incinerator. 'Love, I built this for you!'

My sister laughed so much that the milk she was drinking came out her nose. The incinerator was Dad's Taj Mahal.

Mum couldn't turn it down, and so a compromise between burning and washing was worked out. Like some Gothic answer to the Plague or witchcraft, a roster of Incinerating Days was implemented, and invariably they took on an almost festive atmosphere.

'There's nothing like a fire to clean things up,' my father said. He would stare into the flames and occasionally poke at them with a long stick, sending ash and embers drifting into the sky.

I can still recall being hurried along by my mother when she picked me up from school one afternoon, her booming voice carrying across the playground. 'Hurry up, hurry up, it's Incinerator Day!'

All went well until the day of the history lesson at school where we watched a documentary on Russia's Molotov cocktails during the siege of Moscow in World War II. Fuelled by a quest for scientific knowledge and armed with a can of two-stroke, an empty milk bottle and one of Mum's tea towels, I decided to test whether or not Molotovs actually worked.

Against the side of the incinerator they worked wonderfully well. Unfortunately it was washing day, and I looked up to see the Hills hoist chock full of burning towels and undies. I stood staring at the washing. I thought of calling the firemen but decided against it. They would tell my parents and would think I started the fire deliberately and then maybe I'd have to answer questions. It would have looked a bit weird, having to explain why I was burning my parents' underwear. And besides, I didn't want the firemen to see my parents' underwear in the first place.

So I raced and grabbed the garden hose, pointed it at the washing and then realised I hadn't turned the tap on. I raced back, turned it on, and then had to pull the kinks out of the hose. Eventually water sprayed onto the washing. A pair of my father's undies flamed the longest. To this day the image haunts me whenever I have had to peg or collect washing.

Of course I never said anything to anyone about the incident.

My mother was mystified. 'It looks as if they're burnt,' she said, holding up a pair of comfortably sized underpants.

'Maybe the sun burnt them,' I offered.

'It wasn't that hot,' my mother said.

'Maybe you didn't wash them. Maybe they're not scorch marks...'

'Oh, thank you very much.'

My father had had enough. 'Hey! You can leave that talk in the dairy,' he said.

The backyard was also the place for cracker nights and other incendiary events – the Night of the Flaming Wheelbarrow being the most legendary. It was the height of summer, sticky and humid. When sleeping was difficult and there was a furtive restlessness in the air. Two noises droned through the night: my father's snores and the buzzing of the cicadas. They both sang an oddly hypnotic duet and it was only when they stopped that we all heard it. In the early morning hours there was 'The Noise'. A creeping, rustling noise. The noise of no good. The noise of trespass.

My brother asked me if I heard it. I whispered that I had and I held my breath.

Along the landing my sisters crept.

'Is there someone on the verandah?' Laurie whispered.

'It's coming from the shed,' my brother said.

My mother tiptoed out to see what was going on. She assessed the situation. 'Are you going gog goggs?'

'Can you hear that noise?' the youngest of my three sisters whispered.

Mum crooked her head to listen. 'Oh dear… What the bloody hell is it?'

'It's somebody in the shed,' said Vaughan. He hadn't moved from his bed and I was still holding my breath.

My mother turned and went back to her bedroom.

'Colin, Colin,' she whispered.

'You whaaaa?' My father might have been muttering in his sleep but it still sounded like an air-raid warning.

Mum tried to shush him. 'There's someone in the backyard.'

'You wha… You wha?' My father was on the case.

Mum always had to be careful when waking Dad suddenly. Once, in the early years of their marriage, he had collapsed on the couch after working a double shift on the docks. Mum tiptoed up to him to give him a kiss on his forehead. Just as she was about to gently press her lips to his skin, he grabbed her by the throat and started to choke her. 'Only for a tick, love,' my father would later qualify.

'You were throttling me, Colin,' she'd say, gently patting him on the arm. 'He didn't know where he was. Just woke up with a start. Heard me creeping up to give him a kiss and then he grabbed me. He thought I was a German.'

'Sorry, love,' my father would say.

My mum would give him a peck on the head.

My father had joined the army when he was just a boy of seventeen and he'd ended up a paratrooper. He rarely spoke about the war but he did draw on his experiences to offer exactly the same advice to each of his daughters when they announced they were going backpacking across Europe.

'I don't know what you want to go there for. There's nothing to see.'

'How do you know?' they asked.

'I've been to Europe. All they do is shoot at you.'

'Dad!' someone would say in protest.

'Who's to say they still won't?'

As my mother tried to make my father understand what the noise was in the shed, I thought we might see some of the old soldier in action.

'Colin, there's somebody outside,' she said again.

Dad paused. 'Does he want to hire something?'

'Dad, it's two in the morning,' Laurie said.

'Lousy sod.' My father was up. 'Bastard. What's he doing in the shed?'

'I don't know,' my mother was close to exasperation.

'Bastard. You lot stay here, I'll fix the tripehound.' He set off and promptly walked into a glass door. He told us to keep down and be quiet. We followed him out onto the verandah.

It never occurred to any of us that he wouldn't go out there and try to protect us. Never once.

'Do you want a torch?' asked Mum.

'No, love, he'll see me coming. I'll take him by surprise.'

We could track his progress by the explosions of invective and cursing as he bumped and tripped over a thousand and one objects.

'Jesus, my bloody toe!' He'd try to whisper his oaths and elongate the cursing to make up for the lack of volume. We heard a heavy, thumping crack and guessed he'd walked into a low beam of the verandah. The whole house shook.

'Youuuuuu bloooodyyyyyyy baaaaaaaastarrrrrrrd of a thing.'

A few steps along we heard another oath, but this time it was followed by a pleasantly surprised whisper. 'Hey, Riss, Riss. I've just found my trowel.' (Riss was my father's nickname for my mother, whose name was Iris.) On he crept, muttering to himself. 'I'll fix up that gnome tomorrow.'

I think it was my mother who started laughing first, but whoever it was began the break in the dark night's dam of silence. Soon all of us huddled there on the verandah were trying to stop giggling

'Hey love, you wouldn't have a machete handy, would you?' my father called.

But we could still hear the rustling in the shed. And I could no longer hear my father.

'Where's Dad?' I asked.

The question was never answered. There was no need. Out of nowhere he appeared in a ball of flame. He'd found a wheelbarrow full of old papers by the barbecue and had poured some kero on it and set it alight. He pushed it in front of him, across the backyard, screaming. He was wearing his birthday pyjamas – a cream, cotton pair of shorts with knights in armour printed on them. Bits of paper flew from the barrow and up into my father's face. His head was covered in a page.

We stood dumbfounded as he roared across the couch grass.

'Oh, my bunting...' said Mum.

It made no sense for a minute but then I remembered I'd been playing volleyball in the backyard and had used some of Mum's party bunting as a net. I'd forgotten to take it down. Dad's war cry took on a sudden garrotted quality as he broke through my volleyball net.

'There goes your bunting,' Vaughan said.

Draped in bunting, Dad pushed the barrow through the open door of the shed, screaming, 'Cop this, you bastard!'

As soon as the barrow entered the shed what seemed like a hundred cats came pouring out. Dad looked around in disbelief and then started to laugh. Soon we were all roaring.

That was the Night of the Flaming Wheelbarrow.

The backyard was also a place of celebration. My brother and sisters all had their twenty-first birthday parties there. We'd drag out the big green tent from the shed, dust off the spiders' webs and plonk down the keg, which would be delivered at the last possible moment from the Palace Hotel at Woody Point. The keg and the mysteries of spearing it with Temp-Rite and controlling the gas would always engage my father and his friends. Dad would yell at nobody in particular, and his crew would mess about giving useless advice that would just hang in the air.

'Maybe you should ring the bloke from the Palace, Col.'

'We don't need that banjo player.'

'You haven't speared it right.'

'Well, I can see that.'

'You wanna make sure the gas is right.'

'Are you telling me how to spear a keg?'

'I'm just telling you, you want to get the gas right.'

'Where are you going?'

'To get that bloke from the Palace.'

'You are not going to get that fella from the Palace. They charge to come out.'

'Well, we'll have flat beer then.'

'It'll match your flat head.'

'Charming.'

A drinks tent would be set up beside the keg and Dad's mate Big Jimmy would be the bartender. Big Jimmy used to be a policeman and looked like he was chipped from granite. He would watch everybody as though they were suspects in some major crime, and his big joke every party was to pour a drink and then glower at one of my brother's mates, saying 'Didn't I arrest you once?' before roaring with laughter.

The food for the party would come from all corners. Aunty Rita would bring roll-mops, whisky and salted nuts. Bowls of chips and buckets of prawns would be sprinkled around the yard on trestle tables, and Mum and my sisters would make sausage rolls and pavlovas.

Dad always made time to engage in his running battle with the music. Led Zeppelin or Bachman-Turner Overdrive would be whipped off and we would have to listen to 'The Mexican Shuffle' or some Tony Bennett number. But for my brother's twenty-first, Mum hired an expensive cartridge player from Chandler's in the Valley in Brisbane. At the time the Brisbane floods were peaking and we didn't know if we'd ever see this much-vaunted piece of new technology. All day long I kept a look out for the delivery truck. Would it get through the floods? Joh Bjelke-Petersen had given us all an extra week of school holidays to help cope with the disaster, so despite the fact that half of Brisbane was under water, I felt like I was way ahead.

Late in the afternoon a van chugged up the lane and a happy man jumped out. He joked with Mum that it'd take more than a flood to stop his delivery. He accepted a cup of tea and went about his business of setting up the cartridge player. I used to like chatting to repairmen and tradesmen. In fact I thought that being a television repairman was about the most exciting job you could possibly have. That someone could tinker with a box of valves and wires and lights in an ordered fashion, without having to resort to screams and bellows and threats to the dog to make a picture appear, was pure magic to me. The cartridge man was no different.

'This, young fellow,' he said to me with a smile, 'is the sound of tomorrow. Soon everyone will be listening to music like this.' He proffered a cartridge that was the size of a loaf of bread. It didn't strike me as looking very modern. And indeed that was the only time I ever listened to music from a cartridge player. It was a bizarre choice – Sly and the Family Stone on one cartridge and Roger Whittaker on the other.

About halfway through the evening, my father would insist on making a speech. He'd clap his hands and in his best speaking voice would start out confidently enough, then get sidetracked by one of his friends and end up assuring people that he could always be relied upon 'to provide competitive deals when it came to cement mixers'.

Big Jimmy always laughed.

At that point Mum would yell, 'Come everybody, let's drown ourselves in champers!' and great bottles of Spumante would be handed around like weapons. Half an hour later my father would be walking around muttering that everyone was drinking his money. A sea of people gathered under the lines of bunting that Mum would drape from the verandah to the gum trees. Kenny Griffiths, a friend of my brother, always said it looked like the opening of a service station. I'd stand on the verandah, looking down and marvelling at all the happy people. The fruit bats screeched with joy and the Christmas beetles bombed and danced on top of people's heads. And Dad would yell in triumph as the keg was finally speared.

My father's mirth was infectious, especially when he was on the roof. You knew when he was getting a bit bored and restless; you'd see him building up to it the day before. He'd prowl around the house muttering and pointing. 'Better fix that up…that'll have to be done… Jesus, how did I let that go…' It was even worse if he caught you laughing at him.

'Listen, you bloody piecan, this sort of house demands constant upkeep, it's like a boat, like a big clipper!' And then he'd be off with his list.

But when he was on the roof he'd have the rest of the family in fits. Early in the morning you would hear him scraping across the corrugated iron, swearing and cursing. While the rest of us lay in our warm beds, he'd be hauling himself, his trusty hammer and his vocabulary of abuse up to the house's highest peak. You'd hear him hammering in loose nails, heavy pounding blows that would make the house shake. Then there'd be a sudden, muffled thud – the sound of a hammer hitting a thumb – and we'd wait for what was to come…

'Jeeeesuuuus Christ Allll Blooddddy Mightyyyyy! Youuuu Bastarrrrd! Jeeeesuuuus Weeeeeept!'

Ernie Patching, a fireman who lived up on the corner, said he used to set his clock by my father's screams.

When Dad came down for breakfast he'd give birth to a new description of a bad day. Asked how he was, he'd scowl and growl. 'I'm bloody lousy, a real black-thumb day today.' And then he'd show us the big black moon rising from the bottom of his thumbnail.

Our dining table took up the entire room. It was a big, long table built for a family that liked food and fights and debates. We all had our given spaces. I sat up one end and as the youngest I watched over the years how the table was buffeted and scarred by battle. Those were the years of Johannes Bjelke-Petersen, of stifled debate and public compliance with authority. But not around our table. Food and cups and opinions were flung with passion and verve. And as much as there was anger, there was also laughter. Abortion, equal opportunity, land rights, the economy and how the world came to be and what it would become were passed back and forth as frequently as the salt and pepper. There are gouges on that table where points were made and arguments lost.

I remember one time Dad asking my brother what he was rabbiting on about and my sister saying, 'He's not saying anything; it's just his nose banging on his bottom teeth.' My brother had his revenge, though, when my sister tearfully mentioned her weight. She thought she was too thin. Dad tried to pacify her. 'Don't worry, love, you'll have a couple of kids and go like a brick shithouse.' When she left in tears he looked around in genuine confusion. 'What did I say?'

It was around the table that I saw contradicting images of my father. He was a man who rarely spoke about what he had seen in his life, but I think what he witnessed in the war and the Depression were never far from his mind. Justice and prejudice walked with him side by side, yet in many ways he was a man of his times. We'd be yelled at to 'Sit like a white man, for Christ's sake', but the same man would be close to tears and racked with anger at how the Aborigines were being treated on the reserves of Western Queensland.

Once I noticed that his knuckles were scarred and scraped. The bruises and swelling were far worse than anything he'd get hurling cement mixers and trestles about. His left eye was pouched and swollen too. I asked him what had happened.

He didn't look up from his paper. 'Accident brushing me teeth.'

I let it go. Later I heard from a friend's father that my old man had cleared a bar because there was a group of out-of-town fishermen who wouldn't let an Aboriginal bloke drink there. 'These fellas made a bit of a fuss about it. And your old man just went at them. The whole bloody bunch. Cleared the lot.' My friend's father shook his head, lit an Ardath and laughed. 'Funny bird, your old bloke. Funny bird.'

I don't think my father could ever really put into words what he actually felt about the world. He would see things that he thought were wrong and he would try to right them. He was sometimes constrained by his friends, by the person he was, and by the times he lived in. Yet every so often something inside him would explode and he'd stand and deliver. He would, I think as the old-fashioned phrase has it, rise above himself. It never ceased to surprise.

One morning my brother offered me twenty dollars to tell Dad that I was a 'Perry Como' – our rhyming slang for a homosexual. We thought it was a great joke. So I went downstairs and greeted my father as he was tucking into his usual hearty breakfast. I acted out the part. 'Dad, there's something you should know... I'm gay. Homosexual.'

He didn't explode or scream, just stopped eating and stared at me. 'You're a fool,' he said quietly. 'You're a bloody fool. I had an officer who was bent as an S-bend and it was his business. I saw him fighting to save men with half his body blown away. He was a fine man. You'd be lucky to be a tenth of the man he was. If you ever judge somebody by what they are and not what they do, then you're a bloody fool.'

A week later he admonished me for not holding a knife like a man. 'For Christ's sake, will you not be such a bloody Jesse. Hold the bloody thing like you mean business. Like you're cutting cane!'

My father had his own peculiar language. No one quite knew where his invented words came from, not even Dad. But it was usually around the table that he'd let loose. He had an array of abuse that was truly incandescent. If you were a person he didn't think highly of, say a bit of a goose, you could expect to be called 'a piecan', 'an arsepart', 'a tripehound', 'a goomph', 'a banjo player', or a 'real zeppo'. Or else you might be 'as mad as a two-bob watch', 'as drunk as a fiddler's bitch', 'as ugly as the inside of a yak's arse', and so on. If he wanted to go to sleep he'd stand up and say, 'Well, I'm off up the dancers to go bo-bo's.' The dancers were the stairs up to the bedrooms. But bo-bo's? That was sleep. Sometimes when he was on song, he'd string them all together.

During lunch one Sunday he saw me chewing on a little rubber toy grasshopper. It was my idea of a joke. Mum had been complaining about the bugs in the house and so I'd shoved this old rubber grasshopper between two slices of bread. When Dad saw me his big head turned and he gave it to me with both barrels. 'Jesus Christ all bloody mighty, will you look at that son of yours! The bloody tripehound's chewing on a bit of Malayan rubber sap. Get it out of your mouth, you bloody banjo player, you don't know what Hong Kong coolie's pissed on it!' Never once was the abuse taken personally. It was as if his explosions were some grand parade, a real show.

My mother, not to be outdone, would throw in creations of her own. For reasons known only to her, when you went to the toilet you were never allowed to say poo. The 'number two's' were deemed common, and so when in Dad's man-to-man speak you had to 'back one out', Mum would insist on us calling the whole procedure 'going goggers'. Where it came from is lost in the mist of phonetic time, but nobody batted an eyelid when one of us walked past and said 'I go gogg goggs'. Unfortunately this language spoken within the creaking walls of our home didn't translate too well in the outside world.

Once when we were all haring off to the football I implored my father to stop. I had to go to the toilet. We screeched to a halt at a service station, and I was ordered to be quick and ominously warned 'to watch my mouth'. I did my best to ask the attendant if I could use the toilet but I was a bit shy and he didn't seem to understand. He wasn't all that old and was doing some study while he worked. One of his textbooks was called *The Web of Life*.

Dad must have seen me inside having trouble and he leapt from the lime-green ute and flung open the door. He tried to make things clearer. 'For Christ's sake...the boy wants to go goggers. Goggers...gog gogs...'

Still no comprehension from the attendant. My father waved a small Redcliffe Dolphins football flag in frustration then tried a more blokey tone. 'Listen, chief, the boy has to back

out a mullet... Oh, Jesus wept, he wants to strangle one...
for Christ's sake.'

Still the attendant stared. Wondering whether anything like
this could ever be seen in *The Web of Life*, I whispered, 'I
have to poo. Can I use your toilet, please?' My father poked
me with a finger. The attendant gave me a key. Dad growled.
'Don't you let your mother hear you talk like that.'

3

We gathered as a family around the big dining table, arguing, yelling, laughing, but usually just waiting to be fed. For about a year we actually said grace. Then somehow the pre-dinner thanks changed. All of us, including my father, would grab our knives and forks and bang them on the table chanting, 'We want to eat. We want to eat.' Mum would stare at us from the kitchen.

'What's for dinner?' we'd cry.

'Boiled, bleeding bloody arseholes,' Mum would say.

Then we'd all carry on as usual.

Above the table was a long, thin fluorescent light. One of Dad's friends – a violently red-haired, cross-eyed electrician with a thick Scottish accent called Neil – installed it. My father would look up at the light and shake his head. 'That's a bloody miracle, that is.'

This lasted for about two weeks. After that the light wouldn't work without someone fiddling with the tube. In the middle of a meal one of us would casually get up from our chair and climb onto the table and slowly rotate the tube. Most times it would come on and so we thought this was the normal way you switched on a fluorescent light.

But sometimes it just refused to work. Advice would be given.

'Just tap it.'

'I *am* tapping it.'

'Tap the bloody thing.'

'Colin.'

'Well, for Christ's sake. A man's been working all day and all I ask is to have a bit of bloody light to eat by.'

'Just tap it a little...no need to thump it.'

'You've got no idea, have you? No bloody idea whatsoever.'

'I beg your pardon.'

'You can't even turn on a light.'

'Do I have to get out of my chair?'

'Mind my dinner.'

'Piecan.'

Sometimes we'd all be up on the table trying to fix it.

A young lad who was keen on my sister Corby popped around to find us all standing on the table. As he walked in my father whispered, 'Dance, dance, for Christ's sake.' We started to dance, even Corby.

The young admirer, who I think was named Lex and was manager of the Kentucky Fried Chicken shop down the street, walked in to find a table of dancing people.

'Hallelujah! Hallelujah!' cried Dad.

We never saw much of Lex after that.

Playing with a fluorescent tube was ridiculous and probably dangerous. But as my father once pointed out, most traditions are born out of accident and not design, and they're usually a bit ridiculous and dangerous. So that light became a sociological metaphor for life instead of just a crappy piece of wiring.

One night I was a little rough with tradition and as I tapped the tube it fell and exploded all over the table and my mother. She looked at me and yelled 'Typical!' She didn't say, 'Oh, you've broken the light,' or 'My God, I'm covered in shards of splintered glass.' She didn't scream in pain and shock. She yelled, 'Typical!' I thought this was funny and started to laugh. 'I don't know why you are laughing, you stupid boy,' she said. 'You can't even turn on the light.'

Later when this would come up in conversation, I would say to my parents that the process of switching the light on in this manner was a pointless waste of time.

Mum and Dad would look at each other and smile.

'Oh, here we go,' Mum would say, nodding.

'Jesus Christ, you are a silly bloody mug,' Dad would add. 'Can't switch on a light and I'm supposed to listen to you.' Then he'd shake his head and sniff.

This sort of exchange summed up my parents' attitude to families and parenting. It was generally a case of 'us against them'. They knew better and even if their advice made no sense at all it was to be taken as the given way of doing things.

If they were questioned, you would invariably be answered with my father staring at you and saying, 'Oh, yeah...and I'm supposed to listen to you am I?'

The table was where we'd meet and greet, celebrate and cry. On special occasions Mum would stretch her best freshly bleached bedsheets across the table and a great billowing sail was the sign that a real feast was to come. We would take up our positions: me at one end, Corby at the other, Rhianon to my left, and Vaughan to my right. Mum sat in between Vaughan and Dad. Opposite Dad sat my eldest sister Laurie. We kept this seating arrangement for years. Even now when husbands and wives and children try to push in, they are told that they're sitting in 'my place'.

It was an interesting place to have a meal. Rhian had the endearing habit of humming and singing as she ate, while my father would endlessly exclaim and sigh and then mutter that it didn't matter. At the end of each meal he would burst into applause. Laurie and Vaughan would bait each other and I'd try to feed bits of food to the dog on the sly.

One night started off with my father sitting on our cat, Barney. Now when Dad sat down he would simply collapse onto a chair, and so he didn't so much sit as hurl his arse on top of the unsuspecting and snoozing cat. No sooner had he sat than he sprang up on the table panting and swearing, and Barney had taken off through a window. My father's head was crushed against the ceiling, and his red and orange Makita power tool cap was squashed down over his ears and nose.

The sounds of Barney's howl and Dad's ear-splitting scream barely raised an eyebrow from my mother.

'Who put the cat there? Who put the bloody cat there?' he cried.

'Poor Barney,' said my mother softly.

'Poor Barney, my arse. What about me? I could have caught something.' Dad was still standing on the table.

'What would you have caught off the cat?' asked one of my sisters.

'You had his head up your bum, Dad,' Vaughan pointed out.

'Hey, heY, hEY, HEY, HEY!' Dad yelled. Vaughan was given the Ascending Hey. A scream of 'heys' that quickly rose in tone and volume. Once he had started my father would use one of these heys to punctuate other people's conversation.

'Well you di –'

'Hey!'

'I'd be more –'

'Hey!'

'worried –'

'Hey!'

'about Barney –'

'Hey!'

'Poor Barney,' said mother again.

'Hey!'

My father looked over to her. 'What's up, Riss?'

She didn't answer. He looked at us. 'What's wrong with your mother?' Then he looked back to Mum. 'Riss?'

My mother stood at the stove poking sausages with a fork. 'I've got no identity.'

'You what?' My father stared at her, rubbing his elbow, his Makita cap obscuring his eyes. Forcing him to hold his head back.

'Mum, call the dog,' said Corby.

Mum called the dog then turned back to the sausages. 'I've got no identity.'

The sausages spat back at her.

My father sighed and climbed down from the table. 'Jesus, here we bloody go,' he muttered.

Everyone was silent except for Rhian, who was humming a Joni Mitchell song. After a minute I began to bang my knife and fork on the table. I was joined by my brother and sisters. 'We want to eat. We want to eat.'

Dad walked over to Mum, put his arms around her and gave her a hug. She laughed and pushed him away.

'What's for dinner?' he said gently.

She looked at him and yelled, 'What do you think?'

They answered together and then fell into each other's arms. 'Boiled bleeding bloody arseholes!'

Outside in the backyard Barney moaned. Nobody heard.

It was at that table one night that I asked a question that had been intriguing me. Where did cane toads come from? This question had been on my mind for a while. I loved living in this house. I loved my family. But why were we afflicted with the cane toad?

45

My father was about to push a mighty shovelful of food down his gullet when he paused to answer me. 'Well, sunshine,' he said, 'it seemed like a good idea at the time.'

It seemed like a good idea at the time. There are many moments throughout history of which this can be said. The Leyland P76, Napoleon invading Russia, making Kim Hughes the Australian cricket captain, buying a loved-one a K-Tel record selector for Christmas. They were all good ideas at the time. Few of these brainstorms, however, match what happened at Gordonvale, in Far North Queensland in June 1935, when *Bufo Marinus* (the cane toad's Latin name) was unleashed.

Yes, dear old *Bufo*. It sounds like a name a boxer or a rap artist might have. But no, it is the name that people who are clever at science give to cane toads. It was also a person who was clever at science who thought it might be a good idea to let loose old *Bufo* on the Australian landscape, but I won't go into that. I will say, though, that whoever that scientist was would probably drive a P76, think that Kim Hughes should still be the captain of Australia and have an extensive collection of record selectors.

Bufo was supposed to destroy the beetles that were damaging the sugar cane crops. Not a chance. *Bufo* couldn't give a stuff about the beetle; he'd found paradise and he gorged on Australia's native fauna like a hungry teenager with a bucket full of combo vouchers does at McDonald's.

So *Bufo's* thrived here, indeed he's partied long and hard. I could go into a detailed scientific history of *Bufo* but I'll leave that to the people who are clever at science.

Our relationship has never been a healthy one. I hate *Bufo* and *Bufo* has always treated me like the sugar cane beetles, he couldn't give a stuff. Cane toads just go about their business and when I come into contact with them I just go to pieces.

I still do the Toad Dance when I walk up Mum's driveway at night. Back when I was a kid it might have been cute, now it's plain pathetic. The plan is to run and make yourself as light as possible, so if you happen to step on a toad you don't feel it. It makes no difference if I'm barefoot or wearing shoes. The idea of stepping on a cane toad fills me with spasms of terror. Watching a fully grown man with a seasonally adjusted weight of about 90 kilograms bounding about on the balls of his size twelve feet and then running, shrieking up his mother's drive, is one of the summer sights to which the neighbours have grown accustomed.

Walking the summer streets I attempted to be a little more sedate. I usually failed.

Once, in the middle of what should have been a romantic teenage nighttime stroll, *Bufo* appeared. My date was a girl called Morag and she interrupted my preamble to romance with a question.

'Why,' she demanded, 'are you walking so strangely?'

'Strangely?'

'Like a blind man in a mine field,' she said.

My answer was a perplexed and horrified, 'Toads! Toads!' I looked at her as if she was an idiot. Why couldn't she understand?

Our romance never blossomed.

I've since learned the male cane toad will try to mate with almost anything, even gold fish. Perhaps toads and humans aren't so different; this particular characteristic reminds me of a few actor friends of mine. Platonic friends, of course.

I wasn't the only one in my family who didn't like *Bufo*. At night we would sit and comment on the toads that would balefully glare at us through the big glass doors. Occasionally one would burst through the house's defences and my family's voice would be as one, crying like the pioneers in the wagon trains being attacked in an old Western movie. Though instead of it being 'Indians', the cry of horror would be 'Toads! Toads!'

Mum was usually the one lumbered with capturing the slimy creatures. I don't know why. Her lot in life, I guess, just like she was expected to call the dog. Cane toads were her area of expertise. We'd help of course, screaming advice and encouragement from on top of chairs and tables. Mum didn't really need any assistance, and like a true professional she'd soon round up the unwelcome visitor with her trusty broom and ice-cream container. One night when the alarm went up, Mum turned to us white-faced and called for a bucket. A bucket? Dad got down from his chair to have a gander at the toad. 'That bugger's the size of a bloody Steeden football,' he said and whistled. The toad ever after that moment known as Steeden sounded like a bass drum when it banged against the bucket. We all squealed as Mum's new green bucket from Woolies went hopping into the kitchen.

Ever after Steeden loomed large in my imagination. In nightmares giant green buckets would bang up the stairs and along the landing to stop just outside my bedroom door. Oddly shaped clothes in the darkness would form themselves into a giant toad. My brother knew how to get under my skin and he'd whisper from his bed... 'Here comes Steeden.'

Bufo nearly killed me once. It was school holidays and after watching a midday movie about Harry Houdini, which starred Tony Curtis, I decided to try my luck as an escape artist. Mum happily tied me to a gum tree in the backyard and gagged me, content that I'd finally found a way to keep myself amused. I began to shriek and squirm while my mother and my sisters shouted their encouragement. I think they thought I was trying to jazz up my escape with a bit of go-go dancing. Mum joined in the spirit and stuck the radio on. And so I began to throttle myself to the tune of 'Sink the *Bismarck*' and even through my choking tears I sensed a somewhat surreal moment.

'Sink the *Bismarck*' was a country and western song by a man called Johnny Horton. A country song about the German battleship in World War II. It was a jaunty number that really defies any type of categorisation, although I suppose if you're going to strangle yourself it was a happy enough tune. Somehow Mr Horton had managed to liken the shells of the great ship to steers from an American cattle ranch. Now that's art. It was imperative to find the ship and sink it, according to Mr Horton, because it was creating such a fuss. He was a master of understatement.

I unfortunately began to create a bit of a fuss myself and started to scream, and in fact my mother took my Bismarcking to be enthusiasm and turned up Johnny Horton and 'Sink the *Bismarck*', louder.

Though I was growing faint, I thought that somehow it would be appropriate that I was dying to a Johnny Horton song, for as Johnny in his cowboy twang sang about Churchill telling everybody to put every ship to sail I thought that at least Uncle Reg would be happy. He used to like burping the chorus of another Johnny Horton classic called 'North to Alaska', maybe he could even burp the chorus at my service.

Enough was enough. I screamed louder and I eventually managed to howl through my gag, 'Toad, toad!'

Automatically Mum went for the broom and ice-cream container but she stopped to look at the tiny creature, no bigger than my thumbnail, perched on my foot. 'Oh, the poor little darling.' It was too much; while I sagged in a mess my own mother cooed over a baby toad.

I have no idea why I hated toads so much. I still shudder when I think of going tadpoling in Humpybong Creek and bringing buckets of sweet little tadpoles into the laundry. At the time I thought they were great and much cheaper than sea monkeys. Then Corby took delight in telling me that they would soon turn into toads, bigger even than Steeden. I had nightmares for weeks.

I was always trying to conquer this thing with *Bufo*. Friends would happily pile up atrocity upon atrocity against cane toads – unspeakable acts I cannot go into, and yes, golf clubs were involved – but I never succeeded in truly confronting or dealing with my fear.

In Grade Eleven biology we had to dissect one. Toads had been collected and then stuck in a freezer. What a thing to find when you reached in for the fish fingers! I was sure I couldn't do it and that I'd freak out or faint. I fretted for weeks. When the day came and the toads were pinned on the black desks I peered down at the prone *Bufo*s and to me they looked like the old men who sunbaked spreadeagled and coma-like on Suttons Beach. I shook myself and girded my loins while I prepared to slice through *Bufo*s. I think I overdid it.

Yes, I'm pretty sure I overdid it.

I was trying to be nonchalant and cavalier. Instead I just looked and sounded crazed. I laughed maniacally and waved bits and pieces about and acted like a cross between Hannibal Lecter and Dr Frankenstein.

After this performance questions were asked of my mother when she was on tuck-shop duty. 'Does your youngest listen to that hairy metal rock and roll? That English type music?'

Mum was worried, but Dad had the answer. 'The boy just has to play a bit more sport.'

Yes, *Bufo Marinus* seemed like a good idea at the time. 'At least they give smug buggers in Sydney and Melbourne something to laugh at,' said my father. 'People like to joke about toads and Queenslanders. They know that it's funny, just a Queensland thing. But I tell you this much for nothing, I know *Bufo*. I know he is heading south and west, sunshine. It won't be long before those jokes that are told about toads down south seemed like a good idea at the time.' My father smiled and kept feeding himself while my sister hummed away.

4

When I look back at life in that house I realise it was shaped almost entirely by my parents. They permeated every single corner of the house by the fire station. It was their house and we kids were just passing through. Dad regarded the place as the centre of his empire. Over the years he bought other bits of land and built other houses, but the house on the battleaxe block was the one, his castle, especially when he decided to start his equipment hire business from home.

He'd set up the business with the idea of supplying builder's trestles and cement mixers and things called acrows. He did all right, and he loved being his own man. His catch cry was, 'Don't break your back, ring for Mac.' His trucks and signs were all handpainted and he was as happy as a king tooling around the streets yelling and waving to people. My father was an incredibly strong man. All these devices weighed a tonne. The trestles were measured in terms of their size. It was nothing to the old man to be flinging three pairs of 'sixteen footers' across the tray of his truck by himself and delivering them to whoever was silly enough to hire them. The trestles were his favourite piece of equipment and he'd lean these huge lumps of metal against the house and in the front and backyards. You would find him in all manner of places when he was cleaning them. You'd open a first-storey window about three metres from the ground to take in the morning air only to be greeted with his face staring at you from beneath one of his beloved Makita caps.

'What do you want?' he'd growl, or more often 'You right?'

Sometimes you'd stumble upon him unexpectedly while he was having an animated conversation with himself or Margaret Thatcher or some other imaginary friend. Other times he'd be delivering one of his speeches to parliament. Vaughan and I caught him once on the verandah orating at full voice with a paintbrush in one hand and pot of paint in the other. There was no one around except the dog. Sam sat obediently looking up at him. Sometimes he tilted his head this way or that when Dad became more animated. 'And so, Mr Speaker, I say to the Honourable members opposite, they are...' Dad must have heard us giggling, for without missing a beat he turned and in the same sonorous parliamentary tone told us we were 'A pair of arseparts who've got absolutely no bloody idea. Piss off, I've got work to do.'

He prepared one of his big election speeches on that verandah. He didn't win but it never stopped him going back for more. He loved any election – state, federal or local. In fact, he loved them so much he would participate in them again and again without ever standing a chance of winning. One time after yet another loss to the Country Party in an unwinnable state seat, my mother felt a bit sorry for him, and nine months or so later I came on the scene. I used to wonder if he ever looked at me and ruminated on his lack of political success; if he stared at his youngest across the breakfast table as I stuffed my face with food or was arsing about like some goomph, and was reminded of his defeats. Probably not. Dad's favourite response whenever he was asked why he kept standing was simple (and by now familiar).

'A man's got to have a hobby.'

I often asked him why he loved elections so much. 'I'll tell you one day, sunshine, when you're old enough to understand.' And then almost as an afterthought he'd add, 'I'll tell you this though, never vote for a bugger with a beard. They're hiding something.'

There was almost something quixotic about his tilting at the windmills of certain defeat. In the sixties and seventies he would stand for the Labor Party in a safe Country Party seat. Perhaps it made it easier that he quite liked the Country Party's Jimmy Houghton. They would often share a beer and a laugh at the RSL. Dad rarely said a bad word about anyone, although I can remember him laughing a lot at 'the poor old bloody Liberals'.

We would hand out his how-to-vote cards, sometimes ten at a time just to get rid of the things. Mum still has a stash from some hairy local council election that she uses for notepaper. They seem to haunt the house and indeed each year we are given boxes filled with his how-to-vote cards. 'For the kids,' my mother says.

'Never take democracy for granted, sunshine,' Dad would say when we went out driving in one of his trucks. 'Never take it for granted.'

Mum told me that early in his electioneering days he'd go off on a door knock wearing his one good tie and his one good white shirt that she'd bleached for him, and come back ruffled and dishevelled. 'It can get a bit willing out there, love,' he'd say. On occasion he'd even end up getting in a blue with somebody about his politics, or he'd see some domestic tiff and feel that he had to step in. 'You never hit a woman, ever. You hit a woman and you're lower than a snake's belly.' Sometimes he'd have helped somebody change the oil in their car or build a wall. It was a hobby.

In Dad's office (the room with the door that never opened), squashed in between assorted sanders and tools, was a glass beaker with black, gold and silver stripes around it. Dad called it 'Gough's Jug'. Gough Whitlam had visited Redcliffe in the early sixties, when he was the deputy leader of the Labor Party. Mum had raced out and bought a Woolies special set of beaker and tumblers in case the great man needed to wet his lips. The glasses had long since shattered into time but 'Gough's Jug' had been preserved as a family heirloom.

I asked Dad once what he was like. 'Sunshine, he spoke well and was pretty tall...' He stopped and pondered for a moment. 'He wore his pants very high.' He shook his head. 'Bugger me, he was a choko Charlie.'

'That's it?' I asked.

'He wore a lot of Brylcreem...' But before he could finish I could hear that tune in my head. I asked him if Gough ever wore a safari suit. My old man looked at me as if I were a fool. I hummed the 'Tijuana Taxi' tune. He continued to look at me as if I were a fool. 'Piecan.'

Not everyone my father met in his political journeying was lifted from the history books, though. Charles Stewart-Macdonald should have been in a history book; he certainly tried hard enough to get in one. He was English I think, and hinted that his name was a member of the heraldry of England. He proudly displayed this connection by handpainting his family's coat of arms on the driver's door of his caramel Valiant Safari station wagon. Aside from always dressing in a matching caramel safari suit, the only other distinguishing thing about him was that he always wore a neckbrace. An ongoing insurance claim, apparently.

'They watch me all the time,' he'd say. 'They photograph me. They wait to see if I don't have it on. You can't be too careful.'

Later, he added a steel walking cane to his ensemble and would come around and talk to Dad about politics and his tilt at the forthcoming aldermanic election campaign. It would take him forever to get out of his big boxy car, struggling with his cane, which would get caught on Dad's trestles and wheelbarrows. His insurance brace stretched his neck to breaking point. It was so elongated that when he spoke he could hardly move his lips and he ended up sounding like a very bad ventriloquist.

'Ha yo, eees ya daa iiin?' he'd gurgle.

My father would come out and chat and walk him round to the back of the shed. Once I saw Dad giving him some money. Charles was gurgling something but the old man stopped him with a big pat on the back. 'For Christ's sake, Charley, don't worry about it. Get some nice food on the table and something for your missus.' Dad looked up and saw me watching. 'Go and do something useful, will you, we're talking politics.'

I nodded and shuffled off to occupy myself on the verandah.

Dad was a soft touch but he hated people knowing it.

'He just doesn't like seeing people go without,' Mum would say.

That night at the dinner table he sat morosely munching his food, before sighing deeply and saying to nobody in particular, 'Why'd we fight a bloody war? Folk shouldn't go without.'

But the next day when the special election issue of the local paper arrived he erupted. 'Holy bloody bleeding Moses!' As his big hands pawed at the 'Meet the Candidates Special' he didn't know whether to laugh or cry. A list of local real estate salesmen, plumbers and small businessmen who listed their hobbies as international affairs were joined by Charles Stewart-Macdonald in his safari suit and neckbrace. His occupation was listed as 'an unemployed actor, dancer and housepainter'.

'That's one for the history books, all right,' Dad grumbled, and then a second later roared with laughter. 'Mad bugger; well, he's having a go and that's the main thing.'

In the end Charley was happy. He didn't get elected but he didn't finish last, proudly claiming that at least he'd 'beaten an Australian Democrat'. Who wore, incidentally, a beard.

Dad would talk politics to anyone who'd listen. He'd love being out in the lane with all his hire gear, chatting away to customers. Men like Case Yankers and Cliffy Jenkins and Jimmy Thompson and Megsy Bainbridge. They may well have come for a trestle table or a wheelbarrow, but they ended up having their ears bent backwards with Dad's views on the European Community, how to clean up the Middle East, and his answers to the sewage problems of Deception Bay.

I would sidle past on my way to school and stare, not having a clue what they were on about. Case Yankers was a big heavy Dutchman who wore great ballooning white painter's overalls and a straw gardener's hat. He stood blinking and wobbling in his confusion. 'Col, Col,' he'd say, 'vot da hell has de Gaulle got to do with the Kippa-Ring drive-in?'

Dad nodded patiently like an old sage. 'This is where you don't understand, Case, this is where you've got to think like they do, because they don't think like we do. Don't live like us.' At this point Dad grabbed a hold of me. 'You'll back me up, son. What do you think of de Gaulle?' I had no idea who de Gaulle was. I hazarded a guess that he was a football player, maybe a new winger for the Dolphins who would replace Merv Cook. I wasn't sure and my father smiled at me. I just nodded.

'You see, Case!' Dad yelled. 'You see? Charles bloody de Gaulle wouldn't want to go to the drive-in. It'd be completely foreign to him.'

'But General de Gaulle, he ist dead. Hist been deadt ten years!'

'Oh, Case, that's beside the point.'

When my father's friends weren't available, there were always the Mormons, and I doubt they ever had a warmer welcome. Dad would drop whatever it was he was doing as soon as he heard the dog barking and saw the white-shirted missionaries wandering up the lane. He would batter them into submission, and although they may have come wanting to talk about eternal life and its wherewithal, Dad would brush all that aside quicksmart and carry on about Richard Nixon and China and Kissinger and Ireland. On one beautiful morning he had two astounded Mormons pinned against a row of acrow props listening to a tale about Pale Face Adios, the champion trotter.

I never saw the same Mormons twice, and Mum developed a theory that they sent new recruits to my father for him to test them out.

And of course, when my father had no one else to talk to, there was always the dog. When I think of the dogs we had I can't help thinking about my current mutt, Doug, and how not only do we often end up resembling our pets, but we also end up resembling our parents. I often shout at Doug, 'Get down, you bloody thing!' Five simple words. I sound just like my father and Doug is behaving the same way as the dogs of my childhood. He's being a bloody thing. He often stands on a table in my backyard with something that was once a tennis ball (but is now a saliva-sodden grimy sphere) at his feet. He nudges it in the direction of any person nearby. Doug wants them to throw the ball.

'The dog' was a fixture of my life and essential in my idea of what made up a family. There was Mum and Dad, my sisters and brother, and then there was 'the dog'. Other pets came and went but there was always 'the dog'. My wife once had a dog she christened iconically 'TD', short for 'The Dog'. The dogs at the house on the battleaxe block had their definite characters, and while other families might call their dogs Rusty or Pixie, Spot or even Prince, my parents took it upon themselves to call our dogs Michael, Ben, Sam, Ralph and Paddy.

These names inevitably caused consternation on occasion. People would assume that when Dad stood on the beach yelling, 'Michael, get home, you bloody mongrel!' he was talking to one of his sons. Not that Michael paid much attention; he was a dog who knew his own mind. He was as old as Moses and had been around since I was a baby. He used to treat me like a bit of a blow-in. He had a habit of pushing the toilet door open and barking at whoever was occupying the throne. Sometimes it helped move business along.

Ben was a dopey German shepard-cross who we had to put down because he was just too stupid for words. He would bark at his own shadow and walk into doors. One day he came home with a fork sticking out of his neck, courtesy of the strange fundamentalist Christians who'd moved into the

Worths' old house behind us. These oddly shaped people were always moaning and flying huge homemade kites in their backyard. The mother of the house stabbed Ben because she thought he was a wolf. Sadly not even this unwarranted trauma could engender much sympathy for the poor, half-witted animal. For weeks he got about with a white bandage tied around his wound. Around his neck he had to wear a cut-up plastic bucket with a hole in the bottom to stop him from scratching himself. Unfortunately the bucket acted as a loud hailer and every time he barked it sounded like the end of the world. He'd stand at the bottom of the stairs barking at his reflection, booming his stupidity for all to see. Both Mum and the vet thought he wasn't 'quite right' but in the end Mum was philosophical. 'There's always one in every family,' she said.

Sam, on the other hand, was a congenial blue heeler with whom I enjoyed a terrific working relationship around the dinner table. Every meal he would take up his position directly below me and wait to be flicked the bits and pieces of Mum's cooking that I didn't want to touch. This was frowned upon of course, but Sam and I worked well in a clandestine manner. Occasionally he thought I was a little slow and would try to hurry me up by nudging his cold nose between my legs. I usually managed to give him a scrap of food in time, but it soon became apparent that I was unwittingly creating a monster. He growled once at lunch and I had to make excuses for him. Sam came to think that everyone was fair game and one day nudged a cold nose between my father's legs.

Now Queensland enjoys a sub-tropical climate, and in summer it can get very humid. Naturally enough, this sort of weather requires a fairly casual type of dress. Dad only wore long pants if he was heading off to a Party meeting or going to the RSL; most of the time he got about in his ballooning airy Stubbies work shorts. And so when good old Sam nudged a cold nose between Dad's legs, he deftly found a spot where it's safe to say no dog had ever gone before. The fact that Dad had a mouthful of food didn't stop the explosion. Knife and fork in hand, he leapt into the air. 'Jesus bloody Christ! You stupid bloody thing!'

Paddy was a gentle, well-intentioned bull terrier who got hit by a Mini Minor. He got up and walked home and lived quite contentedly for a decade while the Mini had to be towed away.

Someone once told me they 'didn't get' the whole dependence thing with dogs; that they took up too much time, you'd grow attached to them, spend forever and a day with them, and then they'd just up and die on you. But my father and mother loved them.

Ultimately, like the rest of us, dogs live and die, and at the battleaxe block their final resting place was up the end of the backyard beneath the banana trees. Mum and Dad kept their dogs for as long as they could, but when it all became too much they would make the trip to the vet. The vet's offer to dispose of the body always received the same reply: 'Oh no, he was a part of the family.' Instead it was up the back to the banana trees. So evocative was this image of the dogs' final resting place that it became a family euphemism for death and doom. One of my father's favourite warnings was, 'If you don't behave yourself it's the banana trees for you.' Mum always said that the number of abandoned dogs out there reflected an unwillingness in people not only to accept responsibility of care but also a reminder of their own mortality. I think she may have been right.

My current dog Doug stands on the table in my backyard and I think he is getting old. I look at this mad, long-tongued kelpie and think of the adventures he has had with us, his family. He is nearly ten and he's been around our home and a presence in both my children's lives since they were born. Sometimes they cuddle him on their beds. They play with him; he's their mate. Their 'Dougie dog'. But the day will come when there'll be tears and heartache. Dogs teach a lot about loyalty and love and loss. About life.

So I stop yelling at Doug to get off the table, and like my father walk over, give him a pat, pick up his tennis ball and throw it. I smile and say to myself, 'Get down, you bloody thing.'

5

The house on the battleaxe block loved a party and Christmas was no exception. Even today, every second year the house will be filled to overflowing with extended family and friends. When I was a kid Christmas officially kicked off around the first of December. That was when the Advent calendar came out. It was stuck up on the wood panelling that led to the back of the house. It had been a part of the house for as long as I could remember. It told the story of Christmas. Brightly coloured illustrations of the Christmas characters were numbered to correspond to the days of the month. Each day there'd be a race to turn the flaps of the illustration to read the story beneath. In one of the pictures, Mary, the Holy Mother, was holding hands with Joseph and was telling him something. Joseph was holding a hammer and looked like he was about to hit her with it. He looked a bit cross-eyed and simple. Mum said it was no wonder he believed what she told him. Vaughan said he looked like the big cross-eyed electrician who put in the fluorescent light tube above the table.

The caption read, 'Mary told Joseph she was with child. They must travel to Bethlehem.' It was an interesting take on things. Mary gets pregnant and tells poor stupid Joseph the carpenter-cum-electrician that it's an immaculate conception. And he believes her. No wonder he wanted to hit her.

'He's the sort of bloke who'd live in Kippa-Ring,' my father said.

The second day was even better. Under a pretty drawing of a lamb playing with a laughing child was the caption, 'King Herod ordered all baby boys to be killed.' Other kids had Advent calendars that had chocolates underneath. We had a soap opera-cum-Gothic nightmare.

But day by day I'd be drawn in. I would go to school and think about that story. Herod fascinated me. Kings were always so paranoid in these tales. They had so much power and control and yet a mere whisper in their ear about a pretender to the throne would send them off into the spirals of lunatic schemes. I once asked my Uncle Reg about Herod.

'He was a bad egg. He did in Johnny Baptist.' At first I wasn't sure who he was talking about, but Uncle Reg assured me this was so. I soon realised that it was John the Baptist from the Bible stories from our religious instruction class. Uncle Reg made him sound like some boxer from *TV Ringside*.

'Salami danced and Herod got all hot and bothered and lopped off the poor bugger's head.' Uncle Reg shook his own head. 'Stuck it on a meat tray.'

Dad laughed. 'Probably would've sold better than a chook raffle at a Party fundraiser!'

Herod. It wasn't a name you heard very often, and on a whim, at a cricket sign-on, I decided to rechristen myself Herod McInnes. Kenny Slingsby, the fellow conducting the sign-on, just stared at me. Later in the morning he read out the teams: 'Trevor, Craig, Gordon, Stephen, Kelvin, Jeff... Herod... Gavin, Bernie, Graham. And Errol.' 'Herod' sort of hung in the air. For years after Kenny continued to call me Herod. He ended up working for the local council and every time Mum went in to pay the rates he'd ask her, 'How's Herod going? Still playing cricket?'

'I wonder if he belongs to one of those funny churches,' she later remarked.

I said nothing.

My favourite character in the Advent calendar was the innkeeper, and I told Dad this one morning. He seemed to be vaguely interested.

'Why's that, sunshine?'

'Well, he gave them shelter when nobody else would. He was kind to them.'

My father stared at me for quite a while. He rolled his tongue around his mouth. 'Maybe,' he said. He went back to his paper. He was silent for only a few moments. 'Or maybe he was just making a quick dollar. You think of that?'

'No.'

'No,' my father sighed. 'Here's a bloke who runs a pub and it's peak season and he's packed out and wants to make even more money.' He was warming to his subject.

'I still think he was kind to them.' I stood up for the innkeeper.

'Look, here's these two poor buggers on the back of a donkey. This girl's gone and got herself banged up and she's ended up on the back of a miserable mule with this cross-eyed banjo player.' He pointed to the picture of Joseph on the Advent calendar. 'They've got the arse out of their trousers and they're obviously a bit simple and this mate of yours the innkeeper takes them for a ride.'

'He's not a mate of mine—' I tried to protest, but my father would have none of it.

'Don't back out of it now. This turnip gives them a stable. A *stable*.' Dad was speaking really slowly, as if to a deaf person. 'A filthy stable filled with fleas, and you think he's being kind to them.'

'Dad, I just said he was my favourite character.'

'Oh, here we go.'

'Dad, it's a story.'

'Look, you. He charges them twice the going rate, he chucks them in with the pigs and he's a hero. God all bloody mighty.' He lent back heavily in his chair, flapped his paper and snorted to himself.

I went back to looking at the calendar.

Over the years some of the illustrations had been pulled a little too often and some of them had been torn off. They had been replaced at first by home-drawn figures roughly in the same shape as the originals.

After a while, though, the places had been taken by photos and bits of paper that had no connection to the story of Christmas whatsoever. Over the fourteenth day, when the shepherds see the guiding star, was a photo from the newspaper of the Big Pineapple. The gathering of the kings had a photo of a trotter called Tombei the Mist.

This name came from a character in the popular television show *The Samurai*. Tombei the Mist soon became rhyming slang for being drunk. 'He got a bit Tombei the Mist last night.'

What this had to do with the three wise men was tenuous to say the least. Although the idea of them being completely cut and wandering about Bethlehem after a good night out and stumbling into the manger was interesting. Perhaps, then, the wise men would have been embarrassed enough to shower the baby and his parents with gifts to make up for the interruption. Or maybe they just tried to make it a big deal to explain to everyone what they were doing there.

But the image that lingered longest in my memory was a slightly surreal photo of a cricket umpire giving someone out over the caption 'Angel told the shepherds not to be fearful.'

The Advent calendar was an indicator of our house's immersion into Christmas, and as each week passed a new Yuletide event took place. The first week we'd frost the windows and attempt to draw Santas and the like in white sports shoe colouring. Then the outdoor decoration would go up. This was a large decorative plastic candle that Vaughan had pinched after a night out with his uni friends. It was the size of a small rocket and the word 'Noel' lit up along its side when you plugged it in. It was stuck out on the front verandah and became known as 'Noel's candle'.

During the second week, when the calendar told us about the shepherds and the kings following the star, the indoor decorations and the tree would go up. The decorations were long, winding, interlocked chains of crêpe paper, hung in streams from one end of the house to the other. In between them we hung the dark yellow fly rolls, those small cylindrical cardboard containers that could be pulled out to form a long sticky spiral of thin paper. These would quickly become encrusted with flies and other insects and looked macabrely decorative when the light caught the shiny, brittle wings and insect bodies.

Tinsel would grow everywhere like some exotic moss – even the dog would be draped – and great vines of shiny colours slithered over anything that didn't move. It looked like a *Doctor Who* set. The fact that Mum bore a striking resemblance to the British actor Jon Pertwee, who played the Doctor, added to the effect. She would bellow at us while we hacked our way through the jungle of decorations to eat at the table. All the while Rhian would be humming the *Doctor Who* theme song and my mum would be flinging food and orders about and looking way too much like the snappy Time Lord with her weird judo moves.

The tree was a major family event. It wasn't anything like the neat triangular-shaped jobs you'd see on TV and in the glossy magazines. Instead great sprawling green things would lean drunkenly in the corner by the piano. They were all uniformly huge. Each year Dad would scale the heights of the massive pine tree in the front yard and hack off a couple of branches.

Climbing the pine tree was a major undertaking. 'You need bloody oxygen to get up there,' he'd say, calling for a volunteer to be his sherpa. He'd then clamber up the pine Everest with his saw and Makita cap like some lumbering Stubbie-shorted Edmund Hillary. We'd point out which branch we thought was best or at the very least small enough to fit into the house. Whoever's branch Dad chose would have the tree named after them. Corby's was the biggest but the one that caused the most trouble was Dad's. Dad's Tree would fall on people, as if it had a mind of its own. Perhaps 'fall' is too random a word, 'leapt' is more appropriate. I'd never turn my back on the thing. It was like some monster from *Lost in Space*. 'I don't trust that tree, Colin,' Mum would roar, sounding and looking more like Doctor Who than ever as she handed out the fish fingers like some bad BBC scientific prop. Dad's Tree certainly had something about it. Dogs would bark at it for no reason. People would look twice at the looming crook-backed monster and Dad became more and more defensive of the tree. 'Will you leave the poor bloody thing alone, it's not doing anyone any harm.' But the tree did seem to take set against people. It was like an old actor being made up; fussing and flinging away the decorations it didn't like; never sitting still, never behaving.

Decorating any tree was always a rather haphazard affair and this tree, being so bad-tempered, was even more so. We were all very particular to start with, the shiny silver and red birds were gently clipped onto branches. But much like the Advent calendar, as time passed the odder the decorations became. Some of my old plastic soldiers were wrapped in little coloured bits of clothing and hung on the tree. They looked quite festive. Somehow though, on closer inspection, perhaps they weren't quite suitable. A skinny shepherd/soldier gazed up at the angel through plastic binoculars while a crouching king, who at first appeared to be engaged in the act of supplication, was in fact speaking into his portable radio calling in the artillery. From different branches shepherds and angels took aim and threw grenades at each other.

The decorations on Dad's Christmas Tree looked like the mock up of some battle. My father took one look and declared 'It looks like the Golan Heights.' At first I thought he meant a suburb out west or even a high school. But my father told me it was a place 'where poor buggers fought over scraps of land to make a home'. At that time, in the early seventies, the Golan Heights was a battle ground in the Middle East. My father stared at the tree and shook his big head. 'Poor buggers, the lot of them. Black, white or brindle you shouldn't have to die for your land these days.'

After that comment the unfortunate tree was given its name: Golan. And so when it fell over or attacked somebody the cry went up, 'Golan's done it again.' But still my father protected Golan. Like some owner of a wayward stallion, only

Dad could see the true worth of his beast. After the tenth time Golan had fallen on top of Aunty Rita and her big dopey dog, a leaping Weimaraner called Bruno, Aunty Rita had it out with my father,

'Colin, you really should do something about this tree, it's wild.'

'It's your dog, he was barking at Golan.'

'Colin.'

'Golan.'

'What?'

'Golan.'

'Colin!'

'His name is Golan.'

'What?'

'He started it. Golan was just sticking up for himself.'

I never knew whether my father was serious or not but, whatever the truth, Golan had pushed its luck once too often. The upshot of this latest transgression was that he was trussed up in the corner like Hannibal Lecter. Seething and straining at his bonds to try to wreak havoc on present givers and innocent bystanders.

The end of any Christmas tree is a quietly sad moment. As the tree is disrobed of its decorations it's dragged out the back to the incinerator. A rather ignoble end. Like some fallen monarch dragged off for execution. Even though it is just a branch of a tree, the magic of Christmas imbued it with a personality, an emotional depth that added a sweet melancholy to the festive season. It was a passing, of time.

Golan's exit was an oddly moving affair. Dad insisted that he do it. After we had taken the decorations off Golan and after Golan had managed to inject his pine needles under the various fingernails of we children, Dad slowly unwrapped Golan from his ropes. The tree sprang on top of my father like a lion on top of Tarzan. A muffled 'Jesus Wept' could be heard. There was a brief struggle and then my old man up-ended Golan and dragged him out through the house. As he was yanked on his final journey, Golan's fronds managed to drag cups from tables and pictures from walls. It was akin to seeing a falling mountaineer scrabbling with mad fingertips at the rocks as he plunges downwards.

'He's a swine right to the end,' muttered my mum through clenched teeth.

'Poor old Golan,' my father said as he started to stick the tree into the incinerator. Golan didn't like to go. He seemed to jump back up and out of the fire.

'Come on, mate,' Dad murmured as he poked the wayward fronds into the flames. This lasted a while and we all watched mournfully. But the tree didn't want to go and in the end Dad's patience ran out. The Age of Golan ended with my father yelling into the incinerator, over our giggles, 'Get in there, you bastard, and don't come out!'

Christmas is a time for giving, and every year beneath our tree, mysteriously wrapped in bright paper and ribbon, were the presents. But along with the excitement there was always the question, What do we do with the bad ones? What if the wait is the best part and the unveiling of your gift leaves you dumbfounded? What happens when the present is unwrapped and then unwanted?

This is a tip: most bad Christmas presents come under the heading of 'clothing', if you can call them that. No matter what you are given, you should at least parade the articles on the very day you receive them. This way you can display a show of gratitude as well as reminding everyone who the idiot was who gave you the mess you are wearing. Undoubtedly T-shirts, underpants and socks rank highly in the bad Christmas present stakes. There was a tradition in our family that any shirt you are given must be vile, striped and ill-fitting. I have a tremendous back catalogue of just such fascinating fashion statements locked away in my memory. Photo albums attest to the fact that one year my Aunty Rita had a boon time with the striped T-shirts from Woolies. Every member of the family was dressed in such a creation. We looked like a collection of oddly shaped and sized garage roller doors.

One Christmas I did my shopping at an army disposals store and bought Mum an inflatable life vest. Now she did well when she received the present, although she did take a while to collect her thoughts.

'Oh, that's lovely dear...it's...lovely.' She popped it on, pulled the toggle, inflated herself, then had a few drinks and spent the rest of the day blowing the whistle on the hour.

There would be gifts of vile bottles of alcohol that would ruin your liver just reading the label; aftershave that burned like battery acid; out-of-date chocolates from strange-sounding European principalities; incomplete hobby kits with which you'd always end up super-glueing your fingers together; books that we'd already read (or never would); and music that we'd never play: *The Royal Marines Band play Barry Manilow* for example, or John Laws's poetry recordings.

One year earned the name the 'K-Tel Christmas'. Every present came from the company that made a fortune selling junk nobody really needed – like record selectors and an exercise system, which according to the blurb came complete with a 'unique device consisting of a specially constructed pulley system'. It also had a 'unique audio record to aid you in fitness'. Basically it was a couple of strands of nylon rope held together with plastic toggles and a record of some bloke moaning while a hyperactive Hammond organ whined in the background. When you tried to utilise this 'unique life-changing device' the only thing you managed to achieve was to look like a prone Thunderbird puppet who was flat-out on its back trying to march with its wobbly legs. Other benefits were rope burn and the happy knack of pulling handles off doors, which pleased my father no end.

There was a K-Tel E-z Tracer; the Vego-matic and the Hair-o-matic, which gave you a haircut like a collaborator in the Second World War. And who could forget the immortal K-Tel glass cutter? Mum liked this one. The device could cut the top off any old bottle to make 'a unique festive tumbler'. On New Year's Day Mum had been at work and with help from us kids had made a set of 'unique festive tumblers' out of large beer bottles. Unfortunately someone (my sister insists it was me) forgot to sand the rims of the tumblers. As a result the Lord's name was cried out in vain and many lips were cut. Dad said we all looked like The Joker from *Batman*. On a more mysterious note, Aunty Rita said that it was dangerous because we might swallow shards of glass 'like in the Rock Hudson movie'. The rest of the afternoon was spent picking glass shards out of our lips and trying to work out which Rock Hudson movie had featured a K-Tel bottle cutter.

One year Santa gave me a board game called 'Flight Manoeuvres' – an 'exciting aeronautical game of skill and tactics!' It was really just an invitation to murder. You would set up your respective airforces at either end of the board, then try to take out as many of the opposing aircraft as possible. The goal was to capture a troop carrier. Laurie would stand on her chair shrieking at my brother, 'You've got that troop carrier! That's it, I've shot it down!' Vaughan would deny this and try to fidget the troop carrier card to some other part of the skies.

This was the real glory of the game: we ended up standing on chairs screaming about bombers and fighters and that awful bloody troop carrier. At that point Mum 'Doctor Who-d' in, swept up the board and declared that it would not be played by people who weren't old enough to behave properly.

Two nights later as we lay in bed we heard her flinging the board at Dad, taunting him with, 'I knew I had your troop carrier, I knew it!'

Good one, Santa.

None of us was especially religious. We all accepted the story of Christmas and would go off to Midnight Mass or even one mass on Christmas Day, but for us the real significance of the day was the way the family gathered together; to open the presents and to sit at the table for a hot lunch in a boiling hot house in the middle of summer. For some reason, these events were taped on a recorder and then played back later in the day. We would laugh as we listened to ourselves eat.

'Advanced Lapsed' would be a good way to describe us. I read the Bible to check the Ten Commandments for communion, and then forgot them as soon as I'd learned them. My mother refused to talk to a woman who had worn curlers in her hair when going to mass. And both Mum and Dad would call upon the Lord and his son often and with great gusto, especially on black-thumb days. All the same, my father regularly said that 'Jesus was a good man; a good man to have on your side. Even if you were a wee bit doubtful about his old man.'

But we lived close to religion. After Mr Tibby died his paddock became the Senior Citizens' Hall. Each week the neighbourhood's elderly would gather for canasta and indoor bowls, and the odd rather hilarious musical production. They shared the space with a fundamentalist church.

The great thing about the hall was its bank of windows along both sides. We could have a good gawp at what was going on from our driveway. Friday nights were dance nights. Sweet old songs would be played by an endearingly out-of-tune band. The drummer was usually so far behind the beat that my mother said he must have still been playing the next day. At the start of each evening old couples would walk slowly from their well-washed cars. Retirement cars. The women in smart floral dresses and the men in short-sleeved shirts, ball-breakingly high-hitched trousers and gleaming shoes. 'They were young once,' my brother said one night. 'Maybe only about ten years ago. You just reach an age and *wham*, you drive polished cars and wear your dacks around your ears.'

I would look at them dancing round in ordered lines to foxtrots and two-steps and wonder how this could happen. How do you become old? As I watched I noticed that they glided across the floor, floated with a surety that gave an elegance and timelessness to the wearer of even the highest-hitched trousers.

On one grand occasion they put on a production of *The Sound of Music*. As most of the cast were over seventy it was a rather stiff-jointed show. The Von Trapp children seemed to be afflicted with a ravaging advanced-ageing disease. 'I am Sixteen going on Seventeen' was too surreal for words, and the storm troopers arthritically stomping across the stage at the end was a strange and oddly moving sight.

Wednesday and Thursday were bingo nights. We would hear the deep and relaxed tones of the caller announcing the numbers, then silence. You could feel the concentration of the players. We'd lie on the daybeds on the side verandah and look up to the heavens and see the stars, all the while being serenaded by the bingo caller's own brand of poetry: 'Top of the house blind ninety.' 'On its own number one.' Or the deeply reverential 'two fat ladies eighty-eight'. The bingo caller would roll on and on, and sometimes our whole house would be listening in on tenterhooks.

Mum would be playing gin rummy with her sister Aunty Rita, and would start taking deep breaths and tap her cards on the table. 'Isn't it exciting?' she'd whisper. I thought she meant her game but I realised she was talking about the bingo next door.

'They're going for the jackpot,' said Aunty Rita, and we all listened.

My father went for a walk down the lane. 'Any minute now,' he'd say tightly when he came back in.

The announcer called twenty-two and my father murmured back in bingo lingo, 'Two little ducks, twenty-two.'

Somewhere upstairs my sisters quacked.

'Can't be long now, surely,' Dad said, sounding like a bad actor in an old war film counting bombers returning from a suicide mission.

Just when you started to relax and take things for granted, you'd hear the shrill cry of 'Bingo!' and Dad would yelp.

'Lucky sod,' Aunty Rita would say. And on they would play.

But on Tuesday and Sunday nights the Church of Christ took over the hall. And they knew how to put on a show. While other families would be watching *Sixty Minutes* or those English shows about vets sticking their arms up cows' arses in Yorkshire, the McInneses would gather on the driveway and tune in to the speaking of tongues or even the odd exorcism.

One night a man brought along a huge Queensland blue pumpkin and sang it a song accompanied by a tinny electric guitar. Then the congregation prayed and thanked God for providing food and life. The enthusiastic thumping made the great Queensland blue roll and plop about the floor. I must admit it engrained in me a slight suspicion of religious performance. It seemed as if people required a big event to prove the existence of a bonding spirit. It wasn't enough to just believe.

Full-body baptisms always drew a big crowd. I'll never forget the image of a huge Pacific Islander being dunked by a pastor in what seemed to be a hired portable spa. Down went the two men, and only one came back up. The big Islander. He jumped up, waving his hands in joy. After a while the pastor surfaced looking like a drowned rat. The big Islander got out and a man twice as big got in. The look on the pastor's face is with me still.

Sometimes it was hard to tell the difference between the fundamentalist Christians and the bingo players. Both got dressed up to the nines and most weeks both listened in hushed reverence, sometimes answering back if invited. Generally, the bingo faithful sang better songs. For a while a big, balding, red-faced man called Lofty would bring his piano accordion to the bingo and play between set-ups. His speciality was Calypso, so a roomful of bingo-playing white folk would hum and click their bingo pens to Lofty's accordion trip through the Caribbean. His particular favourite was the slow and mournful 'Yellow Bird'. In a hall thick with cigarette smoke and broken bingo dreams, the Senior Cits sang along.

One year on Tuesday evenings for about six weeks, a man with slicked-down hair and thick glasses showed slides of his travels around the Middle East. It was advertised as a great adventure in the wilds of the world. It sounded vaguely educational and my mother was happy to let me go. The man told stories of an Arab city that had huge fruit trees growing along its streets and how the citizens would be able to pick the abundant fruit. It seemed like such a good idea. The only problem was they weren't Christians. He then showed a slide of a man who wore a moulded stainless-steel bowl over his head. He did this because he'd had the top of his skull cut out because he suffered headaches. The next slide was of the same man without his bowl and the top of his head had indeed been scraped out. The presenter told us that if he'd been a Christian, such brutal treatment wouldn't have been necessary. 'He could have taken some aspro or even Bex.'

Pamphlets were handed around at the end of the lecture inviting people back for more entertainment and education the following week. On the back was a picture of a group of people wearing suits and smart dresses burning in hell. I asked the man with slicked-down hair what hell was like.

He put his hand on my shoulder and smiled. I could see my reflected face distorted in his glasses. 'Well, it's a little like having a pneumatic drill drilled through your kneecap.'

I went home and told my mother what the man had said. She looked at the pamphlet and shook her head. 'These people don't know what hell is. They don't know what heaven is. They scare you into trying to believe. No matter what happens

81

to you, you must never be scared into believing.' She screwed up the paper and threw it into the fire of the wood stove where it quickly caught alight. The people in smart suits and dresses burning in the drawn flames disappeared in the rolling fire of the stove.

6

The wood-burning stove in the kitchen of the house on the battleaxe block was installed by a drunken friend of my father's. Like the light over the dining table, it never worked properly. Smoke would escape from the H-shaped fibro chimney and choke the room and its occupants. Mum and Dad would frantically try to clear the imagined blockages, inserting wires and pumping bellows at a remarkable pace. They looked like some old speeded-up film of stokers in the boiler room of the battleship *Potemkin*. They screamed at and to each other. Often at the peak of anger and frustration they would burst into roaring laughter.

The house had another 'kitchen' out the back, which was really just a laundry with two great concrete sinks and a toilet. This is where Mum and her vast collection of secondhand and mostly useless washing machines plied their trade. It was here that one of my mother's more gruesome tasks was carried out.

For years we had a psychotic cat called Blinky, so-called I think because she blinked a lot. Blinky would sit in the middle of the steps leading to the upper part of the house and swipe at people with outstretched claws. She had a few litters of kittens and every time we were amazed that another cat could get close enough to mate with her. Mum and Dad did their best to give the kittens away, but it was Mum's job to drown those we couldn't find homes for. She'd stand there sobbing at the laundry tub as one by one she did away with the unwanted kittens. Soggy bundles were buried down the bottom of the backyard, under the banana trees.

One time I took a lone survivor, a beautiful little tortoise-shell, to school for show and tell. 'His name is Barney,' I said.

The teacher said how lovely he was.

'Yes,' I replied. 'He's the only one Mummy didn't drown.'

Mum had some odd looks come her next round of tuck-shop duty.

This whole grisly procedure gave rise to another of Dad's favourite expressions. Whenever I annoyed or displeased him he'd look at me and growl, 'This one should've definitely been drowned at birth.' A strong line of black humour flowed in that house. Almost gallows humour. It came from my father. It was his way of coping with what he'd seen during his life.

It was only matched by Mum, who'd preface her jokes with, 'Oh, I shouldn't laugh but...' and then burst into great shrieking laughter. Although I do recall her humour deserting her one afternoon.

The house was renovated and enlarged over the years to accommodate all seven of us, and even though upstairs was usually pretty crowded, everyone had managed to somehow find a favourite bolt hole. Everyone except me. I just seemed to float in and out of rooms.

This led to a rather unfortunate interlude on one afternoon in my early adolescence. I was getting ready to go for a swim with the family down at the beach.

The togs bag was in my parents' room. I have to admit I had only recently discovered, quite inadvertently, the pleasant occupation of masturbation. Harmless enough. But there is a time and a place. On a hot summer afternoon in your parents' room when the family is waiting is not the time or the place. Nevertheless I decided to have one off the wrist.

I was quite involved in my exercise when I had the distinct feeling someone else was in the room. There was a stillness in the air. I heard the voice before I turned to look. 'What do you think you're doing?' It was my mother. Across the vacuum came the words of a song playing on a neighbour's hi-fi system. Johnny Cash.

The song was about a son who had been abandoned by his parents and had been christened 'Sue'. This was in order to make him tough enough to live on his own. The boy eventually finds his parents and introduces himself. In the song's chorus he informs the parents that he was about to kill them. The neighbours joined in on this and kept yelling, 'Now you gunna die,' like an awful echo.

What did she think I was doing? Composing a poem? I stared at her. I could hear the neighbours singing their echo. It was, I think, quite obvious what I was up to. Even I knew I was masturbating. But then I thought perhaps she did not know. I came up with one of the all-time bad answers to one of the most obvious questions. What was I doing? 'I have an itch and it's the only way I can get rid of it...Mum.'

I don't think she bought it. 'Well, then, you should go and see a doctor.' With that she was gone.

Later as we were walking down to the beach, my mother came up to me briefly.

'It's natural, dear, but please don't make too much of a habit of it.' She patted me and walked off to join my father. The incident was never mentioned again by either of my parents but I made sure I told my friends.

One of my friends made me feel better when he told me that he had also been caught in the act by his mother on his 'vinegar strokes'. His mum came into his bedroom just as he was completing the mission.

'There was nothing either of us could say to each other. Mum looked resigned more than anything else. "Oh, Nile, I thought you were doing your homework."'

I asked my friend what he said to his mum. He said they stared at each other for a moment and then he broke the silence with, 'I finished early.'

Save for that one comment, sex was never openly discussed at the house on the battleaxe block. Mum very occasionally referred to genitals as 'Kissy Bits' while Dad called them 'Bad

Jams'. Such reticence was odd because both of them would unashamedly wander around naked throughout the house on hot nights with their bad jams and kissy bits spreading far and wide.

I never had the father–son talk. Instead Dad once walked me down to a hall where there was a family father–son night on. Inside sat all the sons watching an American film about flowers and elks and salmon swimming upstream in spring. Outside we could hear the fathers playing two-up, smoking, drinking and telling blue jokes.

On the way home Dad asked, 'You right about all that then are you, eh?' I had images of great antlered elks headbutting each other, and quivering, straining salmon swimming against the flow and flinching as grizzly bears tried to keep them from their destiny. I hope I didn't have to answer any questions.

So I just nodded.

'Good. Right then.' That was the father–son talk.

Even in Queensland in the mid-seventies a young man needed some details.

Thank God my sisters came to the rescue. In one of their old *Cosmopolitan* magazines I found a sex education guide; drawn figures did this and that. They were all blond and blue-eyed and I think that the father was wearing glasses. I have no idea why I remember this but I'm pretty sure he took them off in a few drawings. The figures were dressed smartly, in fact they looked just like the people who burnt in hell on the pamphlets that the adventurous Christian had given me. The text in the article was written for an idiot. 'Sometimes when Mummy and Daddy feel loving and close they engage in intercourse...' Suitable figures followed right up to birth. The idea that my parents would engage in such activity when they felt loving and close was too much of a stretch. Maybe Dad would make Mum a shandy, maybe they would laugh and yell at each other. Perhaps even have a dance in the kitchen to a Dean Martin tune. Maybe Dad would build something useful, like an incinerator, for Mum. If they engaged in intercourse, well, that was their business. The thought of it made me feel a little more comfortable with headbutting elks and flying salmon. However, I ploughed on and along with the underwear advertisements I got the idea. I had sort of worked it out for myself anyway.

My lack of parental guidance in matters sexual didn't mean my father kept his distance. Not long after the abortive father–son night I'd occasionally hear Mum and Dad murmuring to each other rather cryptically. When I'd look in interest they would stop and smile. My mother would ask if I'd like something to eat and my father would pretend to punch me in the stomach, bellowing, 'How are you going, champ? Fit? Good on ya!'

It didn't take long for me to work out that I was the subject of the whispered conversation. I had my suspicions when I heard Dad say, exasperated, 'The boy just needs to play more sport!' That was his answer to all ills while my mother's was a jaw-breaking, 'Well, you should go and see a doctor!' This was dropped in anywhere without fear or favour or discrimination. To an old woman who was having trouble parking her ridiculously large car at Coles my mother would yell, 'You should go and see a doctor!' To a football referee she didn't particularly like, 'You should go and see a doctor!' To a child in line at the tuck shop who didn't know what to order or would complain about the food they'd been given, 'Well, you should go and see a doctor!'

My suspicions that Mum and Dad were up to something were confirmed when Dad stood and proclaimed after breakfast one Saturday that he was going to spend a bit more time with me.

'What do you mean, Dad?'

'Well, sunshine, we'll do things together.'

'Like what?'

Dad looked over to Mum. She looked back at him.

It was obvious he was going solo with this one. 'We'll get... fit...we'll go camping.'

'Oh dear God, Colin,' said Mum.

'I used to camp out all over the place, I know what I'm about.'

'Where are we going to go camping?' I asked.

'What do you mean?'

'Where will we go camping?' I repeated.

'It doesn't matter where you go camping, that is not the point.'

'What is the point?' asked my mother.

'The point is...to go camping... I'll teach you to...how to do push-ups.'

'Push-ups?'

'Oh, I don't bloody know! Do you want to go camping, or not? We'll put the tent up in the backyard. Just for starters.'

He had another thought. 'And not the big green tent, that little orange thing.'

That night after tea Dad went and got the little orange thing: a small two-man tent that seemed to have appeared out of nowhere. Its pegs were bent and it was made of nylon but somehow we managed to erect it. Dad threw in a couple of sleeping bags and then we went and watched television for a while like we mostly did. He talked to Mum for a bit and took the dog for a walk down the lane. When he came back he patted me on the head.

'All right, sunshine, it's lights out.'

We both went out to the tent and lay down. He heaved around a bit and I asked him if any toads could get in.

'No, no toads in here.'

He yawned.

'What if it rains?' I asked.

'It's not going to rain. Anyway if it rains, it rains... Just don't touch the top of the tent.' He yawned again and threw himself over.

'Why shouldn't I touch the tent?' I asked.

He sighed. 'Look, just don't touch the tent. That's all. If you touch the tent then it'll leak.'

'If it rains,' I added.

'If it rains,' he said.

'But it won't rain.'

'Oh, come on, rein it in, will you? Now night-night.' He gave me a little punch.

'Night-night,' I said.

I fell asleep. It was nice to have him near. Next to me.

I fell asleep easily.

I don't know who heard it first. Rain. Lots of it.

It started softly but soon became heavy, drumming then pounding on the top of the tent. I stared up at the roof and looked over at my father. He lay quite still. I slowly began to raise my fingers.

'No!' Dad suddenly shouted. I froze. 'Do not touch the tent,' he said. He turned over and looked at me.

'All right.'

He lay looking at me. After a while he spoke. 'I never went camping with my old man.' I looked back at him and he laughed. 'You know, I don't know why these things leak when you touch them.'

The light from the back of the house was still on and the tent roof glowed with an orange flare and vibrated with the rain.

We both stared up at the roof. 'Go on. Go on, touch it,' Dad said. I smiled and poked the roof with my finger. Water began to seep through. Dad's big hand swept across in an arc over the tent roof. 'There you go,' he said. A band of water dripped through. You could see it pool and then drop, a glittering little reservoir, and then it disappeared and landed on our faces. We laughed and Dad tried to catch the drops of water in his mouth. I tried to do it too.

'Give you a game of noughts and crosses,' he said.

Our hands slashed across the tent roof and we laughed even more. The water showered down upon us. We lay there for a moment.

'All right then, that's that. In we go,' Dad said and we walked from our two-man orange tent, through the rain, into the house and then to bed.

And we never went camping again.

Dad hadn't given up on fitness entirely, though. 'You've got to be fit, sunshine, you've got to be sharp,' he'd say as he shadowboxed and danced in front of me. He moved quickly and I could feel the wind from his air punches. He'd been a boxer in his army days and a handy football player until he'd done his knee. I could see how strong he was, how sharp his movements were and how sure he was on his feet. But I'd always end up bursting out laughing.

'What are you laughing at?' he'd ask. 'You laughing at me? I will smite you, you swine!' And then he'd go into overdrive, like some steam-driven machine. He would pull his punches and commentate at the same time. 'He's coming back, but his blows have no effect! Is this the end of Captain Canada?'

Dad loved going through the Commonwealth nations for his fight names. It was sometimes 'Captain Kenya' or 'Captain Jamaica'. It was nothing to see him swinging air blows at my mother and rabbiting on while she hung the washing out or helped him load trestles or tables onto the truck.

'Captain Scotland is in trouble!'

'Oh stop, you stupid man!'

'He can't stop; Captain Scotland won't stop until he hears the bell…'

'Oh Colin, stop it!' and my mother would push him in a friendly way.

'Or he gets a kiss...eh?' And then Mum would laugh and give him a kiss and they'd keep on doing what they were doing.

Sadly, though, my father never had much patience for fitness kicks of his own.

'Hey, cabbage head!' I heard him yell one afternoon while I was laughing at a war comic on the side verandah. 'Down here!'

I ambled down. 'Yeah, Dad?'

He smiled and clapped his hands. I groaned. I thought he was going to get me to help heave things around. But it was worse.

'Righto, here we go!' He spoke like he was addressing a football team. 'I've got something here that's going to make you fit, sunshine.'

I groaned even louder. Vaughan had received a chest expander for his birthday one year. It was a series of coiled springs attached to two wooden handles that had to be pulled apart to your arms' length. In theory at least. Mum had bought it for him after he'd been ill. It was an implement of torture rather than of fitness.

Dad had clapped his hands and cried, 'This is how you use it!' He pulled and thrust and stood on his toes and bent his chest like a bow. He yelled and screamed and somehow inched the chest expander open. Veins popped out on his forehead like a garden hose under a stocking. His face went beetroot red. The dog barked madly. My father looked as if he were about to explode, but finally the thing stretched out in his arms. He tried to speak but his voice came out in a thin rasp. 'Now...take...it...and...hold...it.' He looked at my brother.

'I'm not taking that,' Vaughan said.

'Colin, it'll snap people in two,' said Mum.

'Hang on, Dad, I'll get a photo,' said Laurie.

'Oh... Chriiiist...' Dad started to stagger around in odd little circles.

'Over here, Dad,' Laurie called.

He tried to turn and stepped on the dog.

'Don't grimace, smile nicely,' Mum said.

'Ahhhhhh...' He slowly began to bring the chest expander coils back in. 'Ohh...oh... Riss!' he called. 'Hair...hair!' Mum stared at him. He nodded his head down towards his chest. 'Chest...hair...'

Mum realised what was happening. 'You really should have worn a shirt, Colin,' she said as she tried to poke his hair back through the coils. 'Don't close it on my fingers.'

Dad finally closed the chest expander. And let out the scream that told the story.

'Nipppppppples!'

The thing had hung in the shed for years after that. Until now.

'I don't want to use the chest expander,' I pleaded.

Dad shook his head and waggled his finger. 'Oh no no no no. No, not that bloody thing. This is the real number... here.' He thrust forward two large house bricks. 'Take them. They'll get you fit, sunshine. They're the thing for you.'

'What do you mean?'

'Oh, come on. Come on. Sit-ups with them. Hold them when you run. On the spot. Lift them. Go on, get into it!'

For about a week I leapt and sat up and lifted with them down in the shed. I actually got to quite like them. Until I went down one morning to find them gone. I walked into the kitchen.

'Where are my bricks?' I asked. 'Has anyone seen my bricks?'

Dad looked up from his paper. 'Get your own bricks. I had to bog up the incinerator. You want bricks, buy your own... Or use that bloody nipple crusher.'

The height of my father's instruction in life's little necessities occurred one morning as I staggered downstairs in my rugby jersey with my permed hair in a hairnet. I don't know why I decided I'd like an afro perm, but I had one for a few weeks. Corby had suggested the hairnet and I'm sure she was greatly amused by the fact that I actually wore it.

Dad stared balefully at me, without blinking, breathing heavily. He muttered under his breath, prepared to yell, caught himself and then groaned and shook his head.

'It's for my skin,' I informed him.

He seethed. If it is possible for a person to simmer, that is exactly what he did. He clenched his knife and fork as if he were strangling them. Uri Geller couldn't have bent them better.

I went off to the bathroom. I cleaned my teeth and coughed a little. The water caught in my throat. I coughed a little more and made a noise.

My father had had enough. He burst into the bathroom and stood in the doorway, his big chest heaving. He thrust out his knife like a charging cavalry man. His knife was bent.

'You...you...' He built himself up to a mighty eruption. 'It's about bloody time you learnt how to gargle like a man.'

My mother roared with laughter.

'What?' I asked.

'Gargle...like...a...MAN! Get a glass and get outside.' He stomped off.

'Can I keep my hairnet on?'

'Yes, you can keep your bloody hairnet on.'

Outside he stood in front of me. Even as he addressed me I couldn't help thinking that while some fathers taught their sons to drive or to fight or to shoot or to hunt, mine was going to teach me to gargle. I couldn't help but laugh.

'I don't know why you're laughing...a man can't go through life without being able to gargle.'

Mum took a few photos.

Apparently there was a manly method to gargling.

'Right,' my father said and clapped his hands. 'Spread your legs shoulder-width apart, get your head back and gargle. Gargle, you stupid parrot!'

The great thing about my father was that just when you thought he was serious, and maybe he was, he'd see some streak of humour and ride it for all it was worth. Soon we were standing in the backyard, our heads thrown back and mouths wide open, our throats filled with water as we gargled the theme to 'Duelling Banjos'. Or 'Duelling Garglers' as my mother put it.

After this episode I decided to take teenage fitness into my own hands. On a bookshelf at home I found a small paperback – an instruction manual for the Canadian Army's 10Ba daily exercise system. I don't know where it came from, it just appeared. No need for chest expanders, bullworkers or house bricks here. Small shadow drawings of muscly bodies demonstrated what I should be doing. Exercises such as push-ups, star-jumps and stretches were guaranteed to develop a physique equal to that of the men of the Canadian Army.

One exercise caught my attention. The shadow figure leapt into the air and stiff-legged scissor-marched while swinging his arms. It seemed a bit overenthusiastic but who was I to argue with the Canadian Army and their fitness methods? I tried to be discreet about it but ten minutes morning and night soon found me out. In my bedroom upstairs, resplendent in my hairnet and PJs I would leap and goosestep and flail my arms mid-air before landing on the floor. The whole house shuddered. Dad yelled from downstairs. Mum yelled from the front garden. The dog barked. But I continued to air goosestep.

My father stomped up the stairs and my mother wasn't far behind. Dad flung the door open and with a piece of toast in hand roared, 'What the bloody hell...' he stopped and stared at me.

'What are you doing?' asked Mum.

'Exercises, Canadian Army exercises,' I panted.

'Jesus bloody wept.'

'What do you mean?' Mum was interested but Dad just stared without blinking.

'Exercises...from...the book...' I tried to pick up the book from my bed and show it to my mother and still maintain my physical regime.

'What bloody cornflakes packet did you come from?' my father said with hard eyes.

'Oh yes,' said Mum looking at the book. 'That's from the Peninsula Animal Aids jumble sale at the library. The fifty-cent pile.' She smiled. 'It's funny what you can find on the bookshelves. Very good, but I think they're outside exercises and I don't quite think you're doing it as the book says you should.' She then demonstrated what she thought should happen and it did indeed look a lot more sensible and less acrobatic. My father shook his head and heaved himself back down the stairs. I soon lost interest in the Canadian Army and its exercises but maintained my love affair with what could be found on the bookshelves.

It was a funny house. Copies of *Portnoys Complaint* and *Lady Chatterleys Lover* sat side by side with *Tide Times* and *Rugby League: The Australian Way*. Everybody read the books and when they were finished they'd be put back some place new. You were just as likely to pick up a 1953 *Womens Weekly* as much as the latest issue. My sisters, my brother and I would flip through war comics, Mills and Boons and various magazines as well as reading Steinbeck, Agatha Christie, Hal Porter or Patrick White.

It was like a giant trash and treasure stall; bits and pieces everywhere, always changing. Huge paintings by my brother and sisters were hung on the walls along with plates of the *Laughing Cavalier*, Sidney Nolan prints and Albert Tucker's

Victory Girls, together with a smiling photo of Queen Elizabeth. A huge plastic pineapple stuck on the top of two plastic parrot claws stood on a bird stand in the corner by the kerosene heater.

Favourite pieces of furniture would seem to come to life, and Mum especially would become quite attached to them. To my parents a particular chair became Chair, and had its own quirks and personality. She found it almost impossible to throw away her beloved Kettle when its handle broke so Kettle was retired to a special place in the garden as a flower pot. When you asked where the kettle was, Mum would answer, 'Kettle's in the garden.'

Dad said it was because she was Welsh. According to him, the Welsh were all away with the pixies. Mum said it was because Dad was Irish and they *were* the pixies. We would run and tell Mum when mushrooms or toadstools had grown next door and she'd get Dad to jump in and out of rings of mushrooms three times, on one leg. And he would do it, all the time swearing and yelling. Then you'd have to make a wish.

My father was just as bad. His favourite piece of furniture was the television. Or as he'd call it, Telly. 'Let's see what old Telly's got to say to us,' he'd say and on the set would go. He talked to it while he ate. We all did. Even today I'm constantly asked to be quiet when people are watching. But at the house on the battleaxe block the television had to compete with the rest of the family.

Dad would love yelling at politicians. 'You've got no idea what you're on about, brother,' he informed Malcolm Fraser one evening. Malcolm didn't pay much attention. Dad threw his hands up in exasperation. 'This bugger never bloody listens...never. It'll end in tears for this bloke, you mark my words.' He pointed at the television. 'It'll end in tears for you, mate.' And funnily enough it did.

When Bill Hayden was leader of the Labor Party in the late seventies and early eighties my father would will him to do well. It was as if he looked to Hayden as the last link to a party he believed in. 'Come on, Billy, oh, Bill, don't lick your lips, oh, you poor sod.'

'Colin, he's doing all right,' Mum would say.

Dad would sigh and shake his head. 'Poor Bill, you're just swinging in the breeze, aren't you?' And Hayden would go on talking, licking his lips. But Dad tried to warn him. One night when I came home from rugby he was yelling at Telly. 'They're coming for you, Bill, they're coming for you!'

But Bill didn't listen and they got him in the end.

Andrew Peacock was another favourite. 'Oh, here he is! Hurry up and get the ping pong balls and shove them down his throat! Every child wins a prize!'

The weather man was told he was a 'bloody fool' who had no idea what he was 'banging on about', while Mum would say 'Hello' to newsreaders as they said their formal good evenings at the top of the bulletin. It was slightly odd but completely accepted. Telly tended to be a bit erratic. This could be put down to the fact that very few televisions got as much treatment as those that served the house on the battleaxe block. It was only a matter of time before the knobs disappeared and a pair of pliers had to be used to change channels. Trips to the roof would be made in an attempt to get a better picture, and every time we'd hear Dad yelling that he couldn't hear which way he should move the antenna while Mum bellowed back that he was deaf. We would all have our opinions and would try to get Dad to stand in the most ridiculous and convoluted poses, and then see how long he could hold them. Sometimes this was more entertaining than what Telly had to offer.

There were some shows only Mum and Dad could watch. Programs like *Homicide* and the *Dean Martin Show* were for adults only. I was allowed to watch Dean slide down a pole and sing 'Everybody Loves Somebody' and then it was up the dancers.

'He gets a bit blue, sunshine,' my father would explain.

On Friday nights we were allowed to stay up a bit later. This was gold. The night would begin with our special tea. We always had fish on Friday. This took the form of fish fingers, mashed potato and peas. To me this was fine food.

After dinner we would go and sit around Telly and watch *The Benny Hill Show*. It was chock-full of leering, silly sexist smut that completely went over my head. I laughed at the pee jokes with garden hoses and the way that Benny patted the little bald man on the head. Looking back, I can only wonder what my sisters made of the sight and sounds of sexism with a laugh track. The only other women on the show besides faceless breasts and legs were a weird-looking singing group called The Lady Birds, who looked like they should have been going off to play bingo next door.

Growing up a woman during that time was a completely different adventure.

To clear the air after Benny and to get some culture we would then flick to the ABC for some historical drama. Usually about Queen Elizabeth I, or Henry the VIII. This last show had the Australian Keith Michell in the title role, a fact that would intrigue my father no end.

'Jesus, you wouldn't credit this fella comes from Adelaide, would you?' he would say to us in general and then point to Telly. 'You from Adelaide.'

Keith Michell would carry on Henry the Eighthing and I would stare at him and wonder, with my ten-year-old brain, if all the fellas from Adelaide were like that.

After a bit of culture it was the Friday night movie and then bed. I used to get a lot of enjoyment from the advertisements that would interrupt our movie viewing. They were particularly Queensland. I went to bed some nights humming the ditty to Errol Stewart's Bunch of Softies. In this ad a collection of middle-aged men dressed in white slacks, white shoes and mauve bowling shirts sang about electrical appliance outlets. They were the salesmen from the stores and they smiled and sang in their bizarre choir that they'd look after us.

Cross-eyed car salesmen with bad teeth, odd-shaped carpet sellers and hairdressers from South Brisbane, who liked to portray themselves as international men of mystery, all became mini stars in their brief comet-ride across Telly's screen.

The ad that epitomised the era was Big Bill Bowden's Little Aspley commercial. It was a legendary piece of work.

'Ahh, here he is,' my father would yell. 'Big Bill.'

My father knew Bill slightly and so was always calling us to watch his mate in action. Big Bill would appear looking very big indeed, wearing the pioneer outfit of Queensland doers in the seventies. Business shorts, long socks, shiny leather shoes, short-sleeve business shirt with wide tie. His pocket would be festooned with pen tops. His big head was bordered by a pair of whiskers and his balding dome was shiny in Queensland's famed sun.

Big Bill was flogging a real estate development called Little Aspley. He would smile and look around at the land of plenty while shots of rolling hills, the Glasshouse Mountains, Moreton Bay and happy people slowly morphed into each other as a lilting jingle strummed away about Little Aspley, Strathpine, the breeze and mountain views.

Then Big Bill would appear in a market garden nodding his head and kneeling among the produce. Between his legs and thrust at an appealing, eye-catching angle was a huge vegetable. Big Bill would offer this big green thing to the viewers with a booming voice, appearing for all the world like some displaced Greek god extolling the fertile qualities of his estate. 'What a place to raise a family,' said a voice-over, and then Big Bill boomed, 'Would you believe an 18-inch zucchini!'

I can't remember if he winked, but I like to think he did. My father sighed and nodded his head. 'On you, Bill!'

But Telly did deliver two stout (non-zucchini) moments. One afternoon we were watching a dreary war movie, a semi-documentary, waiting for the John Wayne flick to come on. The film was about paratroopers in the Second World War, about the Battle of Arnhem. Real war footage was cut in with a make-believe storyline. None of us paid much attention. Until Mum peered closer and put down her shandy. 'Jesus, Colin, that's you.'

We all turned to the screen. There on Telly was a platoon of mortars dug in the dark mud. And a man in a helmet jumped above the hole and screamed over and over again as the mud flew about him, 'Fire! Fire! Fire!'

It was the voice that convinced us. There on Telly, in the middle of an actual battle, was my father at the age of twenty-one.

I turned to look at him as he sat with a glass of Fourex Bitter in his hand. With his other hand he gently rubbed the belly of our dog. He had a rueful half-smile on his face. 'Yeah,' he said. 'Yeah, not a bad-looking bloke.'

And that was it. That was all he said.

The other Telly moment came on a Sunday afternoon. A Joel McCrea Western was blazing on the box. We all liked a bit of biffo and gunplay, so when the telecast was broken for a newsflash, everyone groaned. There was a massive street march in progress, which back in the days when the National Party was in government was illegal. Dad snorted. 'Piecans.' But as the camera panned across the thronging crowd it settled on a group of protesters who were being ushered away by the police.

And there to the side she was. My sister.

'Oh...hello...that's where she is...' Mum stared at Telly.

'Jesus wept. That's ruined the bloody film,' was all my father said.

We watched in silence and then my mother slowly spoke. 'Your sister's on the Telly.'

There was a moment's silence. And then we all cheered.

Later on, Mum and Dad went to pick her up, and that night we had fish and chips, sarsaparilla and shandies. I think Mum and Dad were proud of my sister. She'd stood up to be counted, even if she had ruined the Joel McCrea Western.

As I sit in the study now, looking at the 'Walkabout in Our Savage Colony New Guinea' breakfast cereal card I think about how these creaky old timber walls are still teeming with memories. This house has seen changes. Like other members of my family it has aged and yet remained young. Now my own children have discovered it.

I remember one time a cyclone hit and as I lay in bed it seemed as if the whole house lifted up off the ground then sat back down again. And then like a ship, just as Dad had described it, it gathered itself and rode out the crazed winds and storm. Girded itself and ploughed on through the seas of time.

I put the card with the man in the slouch hat gently back into the 'L to P' section. I forget about using the phone. It can wait. I walk out through the door that *does* open, out into the early evening. I walk down the lane and look back at the house and as I'm standing there I hear a voice from the fire station, calling to me. 'Young McInnes.' I can't really see who it is under the poinciana tree. He walks towards me. Then I see. He's a little thinner on top, a little thicker around the middle, but I recognise him. It's the Flying Dutchman.

He tells me it's his first night back on duty at this fire station in nearly fifteen years. He's quiet.

'Changed a bit?' I ask him.

'Changed a lot,' he says. 'They've let the tennis courts go, weeds and grass now. It's the blokes in head office in Brisbane. Let 'em go. I was looking forward to coming back too.' Then he laughs. 'I stood there looking at the courts and I remembered your old man trying to play tennis.' He shakes his head. 'That's why I was standing here. Looking up at your old place.' He laughs again. 'It's the same, that house, that bloody house. It's made me day. I'd tell my kids about this place, the big noisy house. They didn't believe it was real. How could you make that up? The house on the battleaxe block near the fire station.'

I turned back to inspect that fine vessel. Still standing strong and alive after all these years.

The Night
of Nights

7

The man in the white dinner jacket stood behind the microphone and told another joke. It was the fifth joke he had tried to tell.

I had another drink.

I couldn't remember how many I'd had but I knew it was more than five. The man in the white dinner jacket had been telling jokes for ages, and every time he'd pause in his welcome speech, he was given to say, 'Now here's a funny thing.' That was the cue for a long, rambling drive along the backroads of the humour desert. He was one of those people who are good and decent, always paying their taxes, picking up litter, being kind to stray animals. People who enjoy a good laugh, but are about as funny, as my father would say, as a bowl of cold tripe.

He'd been banging on about the order of the evening's events and had decided that along the way he'd throw in some fun. He spoke with a slow, considered delivery. I drank with a steady rhythm that matched his, and lent back in my chair, wondering when it would all end. There were only four speakers – a local real estate agent who'd become a successful property developer; the mayor; the man in the white dinner jacket, and the bloke who was wondering when it'd all end. Me.

We were at a swanky restaurant for a benefit dinner for the new local museum on the banks of Humpybong Creek. The museum was the old deconsecrated Catholic church, which the Church had donated to the state government. The government had in turn donated it to the council and the council had donated it to the local historical society. And the historical society needed to raise some money.

'Now here's a funny thing.' Here comes another one.

I matched him with a drink.

I'd walked with Mum to the church through a park behind the War Memorial swimming pool. The park was a former council's attempt to beautify Humpybong Creek. In league with a local services club, they had constructed an edifice called the 'Cascades'. Basically it was a series of open concrete drains placed in a pattern leading down from a reclaimed hill, crowned with a fountain. It was a chunky, rustic effort that looked a little like a hillbilly still. For years it bubbled away efficiently enough and drew water up from the creek and the water flowed down through the open drains that were bordered by some creatively concreted rocks.

A sign bearing the name the 'Cascades' in thin, precise lettering had been burnt into a piece of treated pine. It had an odd look to it. Whoever had made the sign had started out on the right track but, like a child learning to write at kindy, had run out of space. The 'S' had been burnt in upside down, so it looked slightly emaciated and spindly; but it was reassuringly homemade and in those days the Cascades was, for a while at least, a picturesque place to pose for a photo or to hold a wedding. Needless to say, my family decided to have a family portrait taken there.

'Come on,' Vaughan said one morning during a Christmas holiday when everyone was home. 'Let's have a family photograph, with everyone in it. A proper photograph.'

'Oh, the Flagship speaks,' said my father. He referred to my brother as the 'Flagship' of the family – the flagship from his fleet of children. Whenever we set off on some family expedition my father would insist on embellishing the nautical theme by yelling out to my mother things like, 'Look after the Armada, mind those rocks!'

'Why do you want a photo, Flagship?' he said now. 'We've got books of bloody photos.'

'I just want a photo with all of us in it, with nobody missing,' Vaughan said. 'We'll get a photographer to do it. It'll be all right,' he added, waving his hand slowly in explanation. My father had exactly the same mannerism. They would both wave to each other when they spoke – it looked like they were constantly saying goodbye.

'Just like the royal family,' said Mum.

'Oh please, give us a break,' waved Dad.

'We can get a photographer out of the book,' waved my brother.

•

The photographer, who walked with a limp and looked and behaved as if he had just picked out his camera and equipment from a lucky dip, positioned us 'creatively' for a number of photos. 'This looks...really...hang...on...really...is that on? Really good...oh...good...good.' He draped us through spindly trees that bent when we lent on the limbs, and in every shot the fat, squat shape of the public toilet block somehow found its way into the frame.

'Got him out of the book, did you, Flagship?' waved my father as the photographer posed us for a 'men only' picture.

'Just smile,' waved my brother.

I still have a copy of that photograph, with the men standing proudly: Dad, dressed in his Stubbies, long white socks and joggers he bought from Woolies; my brother; my brother-in-law and me. All of us grabbing bits of twig and branch with the legendary 'Ladies' emblazoned across the top of the frame.

The Cascades was a popular thoroughfare, so when weddings were held there, the celebrations were often inadvertently attended by shuffling shoppers, dog walkers and the odd suburban wanderer. Many a photo of someone's big day has some casually dressed strangers wafting through in the background. It was quite entertaining to stroll around the outskirts of a wedding, especially if my friend Peter Bolton's father was officiating.

'G'day, William,' Mr Bolton would boom mid-vow as I waltzed past.

Sometimes Peter would help his father and I'd help Peter with the music. This usually meant that on a signal from his dad, Peter would hit the 'play' button on the tape recorder. On one occasion, instead of the selected song, the hearty tones of Mr Bolton's speech practice boomed forth. Never one to be fazed, Mr Bolton paused, and then sagely suggested to the bride and groom, 'Listen to this bit, it's very good. It's about dog licences.'

On another occasion, after quite a lot of heavy rain, Mr Bolton nodded to Peter and asked the wedding party to listen to this special piece of music which means so much to Craig and Bronwyn (or whoever the happy couple were). The heavy rain had swept through the streets of the Peninsula and all manner of debris had swollen Humpybong Creek. As the toxic water pumped through the Cascades, to the strains of Reg Lindsay singing about Neil Armstrong walking on the moon, the bodies of dead cane toads and bits of eel white-watered down the crashing Cascades, in and around the wedding party. 'That's a big bugger,' rumbled a burly groomsman as he watched the toads almost free fall.

Tonight, on the way to the museum benefit, as a light rain fell steadily, the hillbilly still had long since ceased to pump and nobody had held their weddings or had had their photos taken at the Cascades for a very long time. My mother walked slightly ahead, her two fat happy dogs trotting beside her. 'Do you remember that woman?' she asked, turning to me.

For a moment I had no idea who she was talking about, but only for a moment. When I was very small, Mum had been scandalised to see a woman going to mass with pink curlers in her hair. She was wearing black slacks, a flowery shirt and a diaphanous sort of head covering. At the time, my mother couldn't quite believe it.

'*That* woman,' she repeated now.

'It was a while ago, Mum.'

'She wore *curlers* to *mass*…' Mum shook her head.

We stopped and I asked her if she wanted to come in.

She shook her head again. 'I've got to get my girls home…' She paused, then nodded at the people drifting in and out of the church. 'They're all dressed up. At least none of them are wearing curlers. Off you go. And behave yourself.'

I watched her and her girls disappear into the darkness.

Someone tugged on my arm and I turned to see an elderly man with enormous steel-rimmed spectacles that seemed to belong to a head three sizes bigger than his. He was from the historical society and he spoke very quickly. 'Come on, come in, come in and look at this.' He introduced me to a flurry of people standing outside under the eaves, smoking. I grimaced. The priest would never have allowed that. I didn't catch any of their names, but I recognised one woman who owned a pub on the water and had turned it into a retro palace filled with other people's furniture and memories. It was kind of like a fun, pop museum and it seemed strangely appropriate for tonight's gathering.

I thought of telling her this but before I could I was interrupted by a thin woman with violently dyed red hair and a coarse voice. 'Well, everyone here's dressed up,' she said. 'Whoever is anybody on the Peninsula is here tonight. No nobodies allowed. And *somebodies* can stand out there in the rain.' She and her friends laughed.

I thought of Mum and her two fat little happy dogs loitering in the rain and watching all the people dressed up. 'Is that right?' I said.

'Yes,' said the thin woman. 'This is a big deal.'

'Come on, come on, look at this,' said the man with the giant spectacles.

We went in to the church and I almost crossed myself.

'Look, look,' he said, pointing to the concrete floor. 'Look at that. Look at that concrete.'

'Yes,' I said, looking at the concrete.

'Good, isn't it?' he asked.

'Yes,' I nodded. 'It's great. It's flat.'

'Dead flat, dead smooth and no dust – we got rid of the dust. Have a drink.' I was given a drink by a boy with bad skin, who was holding a tray of glasses.

'Thank you,' I said to the boy, who stared at me without blinking. I turned back to the concrete appreciator. He was right: there was no dust. And no pews and none of the mission-brown woodwork that had laced the old altar. I used to think the stained-glass windows were made of cellophane. The church was a frighteningly modern building back in the late sixties when it was built. My brother said that it looked as if Mike Brady, the patriarch from *The Brady Bunch*, had designed it. It always seemed to me to be rather important. Now it was empty and rather cold. I had another champagne.

They had plenty of stuff to put in the new museum, bits and pieces left over from all the other temporary museums – old traffic signals and house wares, shotguns, shovels, shards of glass, and even a section of the first bit of aluminium cladding on the Peninsula. When the museum was housed in the old bathing shelter on Suttons Beach, it was hard to tell what was an exhibit and what were the voluntary staff's possessions.

But the man with the enormous spectacles said that the old stuff wasn't for display. It had all been labelled and stuck in a side shed. He pointed down at the concrete floor. 'This is where the new displays will be and we'll bring out the old stuff now and then if we think we should.' He nodded and his glasses nearly landed in my drink. The mark on his nose and brow where his spectacles had sat looked as if it had been gouged there with a machete. I remembered that Mum had donated a couple of machetes to the museum. She and Dad had used them to clear the bamboo from my aunty's place; they were historic, she said, because they looked like they should be.

'My mother's donated a couple of machetes.'

'Machetes? Oh well,' he said. 'Machetes. We can use them on a few people in here. Be a bloody improvement.'

The boy with the unblinking eyes and a tray of drinks walked up and stood silently beside us.

I had another drink.

'Well, come on, come on,' the man said, ushering us in. 'It's time to get the show on the road!'

A few people laughed.

'We'll pop down to the do in a car, they're outside now,' said another man with a beard who gently pushed me out of Mike Brady's church.

Everyone except me was ferried in vintage cars. I got to ride in the local funeral parlour's 'comfort car'.

'Oh no,' said the man with the beard. 'You're the guest of honour so you get the good car. From the funeral parlour. The courtesy car.'

'Hello,' said a man in a brown suit. 'You must be my passenger.' The good car from the funeral parlour smelt of lavender car deodorant and aftershave. Outside, the road had a slick sheen from the drizzling rain. The driver from the funeral parlour had a similar sheen to him. Even his moustache seemed to shine.

'I've had a good day today,' he said. I didn't quite know what that actually meant. A good day professionally? Or just a good day full-stop? 'I'm off home now to watch telly. You're my last customer!' He laughed. 'We like to help out and we thought that perhaps it might be nice for you to have a nice car on a night like this instead of one of those old buggies.' He gave me his business card and smiled. The photo on the business card smiled in the same way. I looked at the card and back at him. He still smiled. 'Good photo, eh?'

'Yeah.'

He laughed. 'It pays to advertise,' he said. And kept on smiling. It was a nice smile. 'Yes, we like to help out when we can. Just got the call from a fellow member. I'm in Rotary,' he added almost confidentially; man to man.

'Great. Didn't they...didn't you fellows make the Cascades?' I saw the hillbilly still looming in the darkness as we passed.

He looked at me for a moment. 'You know, I believe we may have. Or it might have been the Lions boys. Not sure.' He looked back at the road. He was a very good driver.

'That...that smell...is that...?' I asked.

He turned to me, still smiling. 'Yeah, I thought you might have noticed.' He nodded. 'Cracked a new deodorant for you... You're the guest of honour. The night of nights. Yeah...the night of nights.'

I was the guest of honour because I grew up in this town.

The man in the white dinner jacket talked, and I drank, and soon I found myself drifting away from the swank Redcliffe restaurant in which I was sitting...

Redcliffe lies just north of Brisbane, across an inlet of wetlands and mudflats and at the end of a long thin bridge. There are two bridges actually – a thin new bridge and an old thinner bridge, the Hornibrook Highway. We were all so proud of the Hornibrook Highway. At school we were always told by boastful teachers that it was the longest unbroken roadway in the Southern Hemisphere. Couldn't hope to compete with the proper world up North, but in the South we were the tops in unbroken bits of roadway. What was so special about unbroken roadways was never mentioned. Why you should boast about it was never questioned. But yes, we did and we were proud.

We had to pay a toll for years – ten cents for the right to enter and leave the Peninsula. Men in yellow coats and peaked caps were stationed at the Redcliffe end, every day risking their lives in the middle of the thin road, tearing off stubs and grabbing at the change that was offered. And all the time their eyes would be darting this way and that, like strange insects wary of being squashed.

Dad would invariably want a chat and had a habit of calling them 'brother'. The men would invariably become annoyed. Dad would enjoy this. Mum said it sounded awful, like something a communist would say.

'Good,' he said.

She waited a bit as we crossed the lumpy bridge, then told my father that he actually sounded like a Christian.

'Jesus Christ! Do I? Jesus wept. A Christian.'

He stopped calling the toll collectors 'brother' after that.

Redcliffe's other two great claims to fame were the fact that it was the site of the first European settlement in Queensland, and that the Bee Gees used to play at Webb Hall after the speedway on a Saturday night. Redcliffe was soon forsaken by the early settlers and the brothers Gibb, although mementos of both still exist. Barry Gibb wrote a very nice letter for the museum. My mum likes Barry Gibb. 'He may have those teeth, but he's a nice boy. Still sends Mrs Filmer a Christmas card each year.'

Behind the Catholic church there's a convict-built weir jutting from the banks of the Humpybong Creek. It was discovered one day when the council was doing some digging work, and a plaque saying 'Built by Convicts in 1824' was erected to mark the spot. It's still there, tucked behind a disused, burnt-orange sound shell – another bright idea of public works, initiated by a council in the seventies in an attempt to give the creek a more 'communal' feel. It was only used once – for Christmas carols one year. For some reason the band decided to crank out Slade covers at full force, flooding the pensioners' houses that fronted the creek. Great, discordant soundwaves screeched and pounded through the atmosphere and there were lots of complaints, so that was the end of carols and Slade covers in the sound shell.

I sit in the swank restaurant and think of those early convicts and how they laboured. How fruitless it was; their construction soon disused and forgotten, to be accidentally unearthed by a council work gang over a hundred years later. I wonder what they would have made of the heat of the days and the humidity of the nights and the softness of the soil. And the mosquitos. I bet that's what eventually moved the settlers on, the mossies. What would they have made of the sound shell and the Slade covers? I shake my head and try not to meld the two images. They must have thought it the arse end of the world.

Three tables down a waitress dropped a tray of glasses. They tumbled onto the carpeted floor and the restaurant's owner–manager, a sharp-looking man with a strained face, flung his head from beneath the bar and tried not to scream.

He held his hands out in front of him, as if holding a bowl, and shook them. They trembled in the direction of the young waitress and he opened and closed his mouth a few times and nodded his head.

The waitress seemed to understand and nodded diffidently in return.

Someone behind me laughed and said, 'He's just had it cleaned.'

More people laughed.

The restaurant owner ducked back under the bar and the waitress bent down to pick up the glasses. I turned away and when I looked again an older woman was crouching down, helping her. They smiled at one another and as the last glass was popped back onto the plastic tray the older woman touched the waitress on the arm gently before sitting down again. I'd seen this woman before; she was a teacher at the primary school I went to, Humpybong Primary. She'd been at the school earlier in the week, guiding the little kids through the craft stalls with exactly the same gentleness. The school had held a fete to celebrate its 125th anniversary, and old students like me had been invited back to wander through the stalls, the sausage sizzle and the fun rides and the memories.

I have a friend who thinks the only place where you could possibly find a school called Humpybong is Queensland. She's probably right. The school is just north of Brisbane and marks the area of the first European settlement in Queensland. The name came from the local Aborigines who must have been relieved to find that the first influx of Europeans in 1824 had given up battling a dodgy water supply and hordes of aggressive mossies in an attempt to settle the area. They eventually decamped to the shores of what later became known as Brisbane, leaving the buildings of the fledgling settlement deserted.

The Aborigines called the buildings *humpy bong*, the European translation being 'dead houses' – not the best metaphor for a place of learning. But Humpybong maintained its connection to the past. As students we were told the origins of the school and an Aboriginal figure, complete with an angry spear, still adorns the school crest.

Although the place took its name from the language of the nation's original inhabitants, I didn't learn much about these people and their culture when I was a student there. I copied from various teachers' neatly crafted chalk writing the tales of the great explorers of Australia – Burke and Wills, Major Mitchell, John Oxley, Matthew Flinders and a horde of others – but of the original inhabitants we were taught very little.

That is except for one wet afternoon when one of my teachers showed us a photo of an old, sad-eyed man in a shabby cloth cap with a brass plate around his neck. The inscription on the photo read, '1913. Sammy Bell, the last of his tribe, the last of his people.'

A girl called Lynne Wakefield put up her hand. 'Sir, what does that mean?'

The teacher was an older man called Mr Henzely. He looked at Lynne and then the rest of the class for a few moments.

'Sammy Bell was the last full-blood Aborigine from the Redcliffe area.'

'What happened to them?'

'They died, they all died.'

'How?' asked Lynne.

Mr Henzely walked over to a window and looked out past the schoolyard and across the bay. 'When we're all a little bit older we might be able to understand why bad things can happen in such a wonderful country. Why we let them happen. We might be able to, I'd like to think so.'

I didn't think it was much of an answer back in 1975, but when I walked around the grounds of Humpybong Primary as an adult, I looked at the murals of Aboriginal-themed paintings on the walls and saw the Aboriginal flag hanging in classrooms where the portrait of the Queen used to smile out at us, and I remembered what Mr Henzely had said. When I saw an old man standing at a window looking out across the bay I went over, said hello and shook his hand. I felt good meeting Mr Henzely again.

It was a strange day; I wandered around vaguely, trying to find my old classrooms. Retracing the steps you took as a child can throw up the most unnerving and disorienting emotions. I knew where I was but somehow couldn't quite navigate my way around. Yet the Moreton Bay figs and cotton trees down by the beach looked as immense as they had when I was a boy. We'd play marbles in and around the roots. I could feel the dirt gathering under my fingernails and long-lost terms for highly valued marble merchandise came floating back. Full size, semis, glass eyes and moonies. I remembered screaming at a boy called Russell Paterson that he 'couldn't golly on a glassy to make it roll further'.

I looked in through one of the school windows and instantly remembered my Grade Three room. It had been turned into a staff room but when it was a classroom, the shelves were piled high with bottles and jars full of anything that washed up on the beach – sea shells, dead fish, sponges and so forth. One day a replacement teacher from a grade above, the dreaded Mrs O'Halloran, attempted to guide me through a mathematics session. She was a tiny, round woman who wore dark glasses and had purple- and grey-streaked hair coiffed into an immense balloon. She also had a whip for a tongue and her voice could cut through concrete.

'Square roots...square roots, do you know your square roots?' she'd say. Her tiny feet in her tiny high-heeled leather shoes crackled on the floor as she strutted back and forth. She was always trying to sniff someone out to test. I prayed it would be a bright girl called Debbie Moss or even better the strange boy with odd eyes who always talked about UFOs and aliens. He'd be a suitable match for Mrs O'Halloran. I prayed and prayed but no one was home to take the message.

'You, the tall boy, on your feet and tell me your square roots!' Mrs O'Halloran strode across the room, stopped in front of me and tapped on my desk.

I slowly stood. I was taller than her even then but she was such a ferocious figure that I stared at her and mouthed nothing in particular. Around the room all the dead fish stared at me through formaldehyde eyes. I had no idea of square, spherical, triangular or any form of roots. I dumbly worked my mouth like a dying fish on a jetty.

'Square root of nine...square root of nine...come on, tall boy! Square root of nine!'

A croak came from my throat and Mrs O'Halloran looked hard at me. I sounded even stranger than the UFO boy. I'd have to say something.

'SQUARE ROOT OF NINE!'

I panicked. Yelling didn't usually bother me but her wail was so piercing that it made me quite afraid and I started to randomly trawl for some form of knowledge, some titbit that would satisfy the woman and make her go away. She puffed herself up to yell but my mind's mathematics cupboard wasn't going to open.

'SQQQUUARE RRRRRROOOTTT OF NIIIIIIIINE!' She thumped the desk.

And I screamed back, 'Captain Cook... Captain Cook discovered Australia!'

Mrs O'Halloran stared at me.

'Apples come from Tasmania!'

It was her turn to stand with an open mouth. I was on a roll.

'My balls are hairy balls and value-balls, said Sam the Sailor.'

Her face went beet-red and I was sent outside to find my brain. As I left I caught the eye of one of the specimens in a jar; a stonefish open-mouthed silently mocked me.

•

In my Grade Four classroom I once got caught feverishly arm-farting by the headmaster and a school inspector. I was engaged in a duel with Brian Christopher; Brian was using the back of his knee with gusto and I was squeezing the palm of my left hand under my right armpit with such force that there was smoke issuing forth. My shirt was half off and Brian Christopher was hopping about giggling. It seemed like a stupid question but the headmaster asked it the way only headmasters can: 'What do you think you are doing?'

Brian stopped immediately but I couldn't. Once or twice more might have been okay, put it down to fright, but for some reason I launched a salvo of uncontrollable noise. Not surprisingly, the headmaster exploded and I was given six of the best; an expression that to this day bewilders me. Six of the best, six strikes of the cane across your fingers, a form of corporal punishment. The way it was said sounds like an advertising slogan for a six-pack of beer or some form of cleaning aid.

Walking around the school grounds on fete-day I saw many familiar faces. One woman had the loveliest laugh as a girl. I would sit behind her in singing class on a Tuesday afternoon while a huge, jolly teacher called Mrs Maclean would bang out tunes like 'Funiculi Funicula' on the piano and pound the pedals like someone pumping the brakes of a car heading towards the edge of a cliff.

And as this girl would laugh her lovely laugh, I would sing.

We had a school band at Humpybong and they played 'God Save the Queen' after the Lord's Prayer at each assembly. Even after 'Advance Australia Fair' was deemed our national song, the band continued to play 'God Save The Queen'. They also played on Anzac Day every year. They were good, but they always played the theme from *Hogans Heroes* as they marched with the Diggers, which nobody thought was odd or out of place.

Suddenly, in one room, a spectre from the past floated before my eyes. Mrs Munt. Old Mrs Munt was our religious instruction teacher and was memorable for many reasons. For one, she scraped her thin hair back across her skull in a tortuous bun that seemed to drain the blood from her veins, and for two, she had a habit of frequently dabbing at her eyes with a yellow handkerchief. She also had very moist lips which matched her weepy eyes, and her cheeks seemed to be the colour of the cream and jam filling in Arnott's Monte Carlo biscuits. She would stand muttering to herself and occasionally to the class. 'It is important to have faith, children. Important to believe.' Then she would dab at the corners of her eyes with her yellow hanky.

Sometimes she would bring in large coloured posters of religious figures. 'Can you tell me who this is?' she'd ask. 'What is he doing?' The posters would show tall, hairy and handsome men in white dresses doing brave things Bible-style; usually signalling or holding their arms out. If Mrs Munt pointed at you asking for the identity of said Biblical figure, the safest bet was to simply say, 'Jesus, that man is Jesus!'

'No, it's not Jesus. Jesus...there are many other brave men from the Bible. This is a friend of Jesus... Who is he?'

I though of Uncle Reg explaining the story of Christmas to me. 'Johnny Baptist?'

'No, it's not John the Baptist. John the Baptist was a...it's not John the Baptist.' Old Mrs Munt dabbed at her eyes.

I worked out a theory about Christianity during these poster sessions: the good guys usually had nice clean, neat beards and the bad guys were either clean shaven or had messy, long, dark beards. I looked at the poster – the man pictured had a beard; long, but undeniably neat. He was big. I knew that Jesus wasn't all that big, tall yes, but built more like an outside centre. I reckoned the figure in the poster was the disciple that Dad mentioned one time when we were watching fishermen cast their lines from the beach into the early morning waves.

'Peter was a fisherman,' he said. 'He was a mate of Jesus. And he was a fisherman.' I looked up. It was unusual for Dad to speak about religion with any seriousness. 'He was a good bloke... A real man...' Dad looked down at me. 'Sunshine, if you ever want anything from the Bible, go with the blokes who are real, like us.' He touched his finger to his nose. I had absolutely no idea what he was talking about. 'Peter was Jesus' best mate, and one time when he had to, when he was needed, he didn't stick up for Jesus. He wasn't there for him.'

'Isn't that bad?' I asked.

'Well, yeah, it landed Jesus right in it, but you see, he came back, Peter. He came back and he came good. He made a mistake and he made up for it. He was real. We all make mistakes, mate, but it takes a good man to come back from one.'

I nodded. 'What happened to Peter, Dad?'

'Dunno. Probably got his head chopped off or something. Most of those fellas ended up in the stink, but he lived well and that's the thing to remember.'

Armed with this knowledge I put my hand up and caught Mrs Munt's watery eye. She pointed to me. 'That boy, yes you. Who is he?'

'The big fisherman. Peter the big fisherman.'

Mrs Munt's eyes seemed more watery than usual. 'Yes!' she cried. 'The big fisherman.'

From that moment on Mrs Munt would look to me whenever she wanted someone identified. I had no idea who the bearded ones were after a while and I soon gave up. I'd look the other way. I had a strange feeling of having let Mrs Munt down. I'll never forget her face when the spitball I tried to throw at Jeff White's head missed and landed with an alarming *splodge*, covering the face of someone who had a halo above him. He was on a donkey and heading for Jerusalem. Mrs Munt looked at the holy *splodge*, turned to me, dabbed her eyes and told us for the umpteenth time, 'It's important to *believe*.'

Standing in the playground reminiscing years later, I must have looked a tad shell-shocked. A current student came up to me. 'Excuse me, do you need any help? You look a little bit lost.'

I shook my head. 'No, I'm fine, thanks. Just having a look around... What's your name?'

'Clyde.'

'Well, Clyde, I've been finding my way around the old school.'

Clyde nodded. Obviously he'd seen a few former students in the same vague state as me.

'Do you like school?' I asked him.

'Yeah,' he said.

'How old are you?'

'Twelve.'

I nodded. 'That means it's your last year here at Humpybong.'

Clyde nodded.

'In my last year everyone asked us what we wanted to do when we finished school.'

Clyde nodded and smiled.

'Well, Clyde, what's the story with you? What are you going to be when you grow up?'

He thought a while and smiled at me. 'Be happy, I guess.'

If I'd had a yellow handkerchief I would have dabbed at my eyes. 'Well, Clyde, it's important to believe.'

He looked at me and laughed. 'What's that supposed to mean?'

'Good question, Clyde, yes indeed. Good question.' I nodded to him, wandered off towards the sausage sizzle and was served by a man who'd been a few grades above me. He was really enjoying himself – it was a great day, he told me as he forked the spitting snags onto paper plates. The smell of fried onions on the barbecue mixed with the salt from the bay breeze. Ibis and seagulls wheeled and squawked overhead and their cries blended with those of the children in the school grounds.

In the 1970s, while renovating a drain in the school grounds, workmen unearthed some old convict manacles. It was big news at the time and was announced at school assembly shortly before the band played the national anthem. It was presented as if the school's connection to the past had been somehow authenticated. Just as I was wondering what had happened to the man who had worn those manacles, and what Humpybong's original inhabitants had made of him, Clyde walked past, smiling. He stopped to chat with a few of his mates and they strode off pushing each other and laughing – two were Anglo Australians and two, including Clyde, were Indigenous Australians. Four young boys wrapped in each other's laughter and friendship.

The sausage sizzle man must have seen me watching the four kids. 'They're a great bunch,' he said. 'Give them a chance and they'll go places. You want onions on your sausage?' He was right, and I felt pretty good. I watched Clyde and his friends. I suppose Mrs Munt hadn't been so far off the mark. It is important to believe. The problem is finding something worthwhile to believe in.

I reckon on a sunny afternoon at Humpybong, Clyde and his friends, their promise and their future, were about the best thing going.

There's a cheer and I'm dragged back to the present. It's our first speaker – the real estate man who has become a millionaire property developer – and he's waving at an adoring crowd. He's well over sixty but his hair is suspiciously black. I sit next to his son who has a sweaty upper lip and applauds loudly and with pride. On his way to the microphone the real estate man stops momentarily at various tables to shake hands and slap other guests on the back. He does it gently to a few older people and I see that it's not just for effect – he's saying hello to people he likes, and they like him. He stops at one old man and says something and they both laugh and shake hands, but the real estate man shakes a little too vigorously and the old fella lurches and knocks over an empty glass.

The sharp-faced owner–manager pops up from beneath the bar, glances, smiles, applauds and disappears again.

I look at the old man; look at his thin hand, waving, insisting he's all right. His hand uncurls and his middle two fingers flick up and down. I'm sure I've seen that hand before – years ago when I was just a boy.

8

It was a warm Sunday in winter and that hand was serving in a beer and hotdog tent at the football. I wanted a hotdog and a can of Tarax. I know hotdogs are a dodgy bet at the best of times. The idea of warmed-up manufactured meat being a treat is something that, on reflection, takes some accepting.

Scrapings off the floor, Dad used to say whenever I wanted a hotdog, before looking at his mate, Uncle Reg.

Uncle Reg shook his head.

'Arseholes and lips,' my father said.

'Arseholes and lips!' echoed Uncle Reg.

Aunty Rita didn't like them much either. 'They're too American, just like Coke.'

'Hotdogs, mate, are just manufactured meat. Made-up meat.' Dad looked down at me. He was wearing his Robin Hood hat. He turned to Uncle Reg. 'I wonder who invented it, manufactured meat.' He sneered at the very concept.

'No idea, Col,' said Uncle Reg with a shake of his head.

'It'd be some bloke, some sharp-eyed scab who had an eye for a quick dollar and nothing else. He'd be standing back, watching other fellas do all the work and he looks at all the bits and pieces of crap on the floor and thinks he can just boil it up and make a dollar. Typical Yank.' Dad shook his head and looked at me. 'And you want to buy one?'

I nodded.

'Then you can get us three!' he said and laughed. 'Who am I to argue with the Yanks?'

'I bet arseholes and lips and sugared lolly water taste pretty good when you're a ten-year-old,' said Uncle Reg, giving me a pat on the head.

I agreed – arseholes and lips and sugared lolly water were fine as far as I was concerned. They were certainly worth waiting in line for at the beer tent.

It was always a bit of an ask waiting in that line. Nobody paid attention to what they were doing – all eyes were on the football. People were always bumping into each other and spilling things. They'd scream and yell above the crowd, straining to hear the call of the 'double sellers' as well as trying to get their orders in. There were two double sellers at work at the footy games – one was an older bloke of about sixty with grey hair and a moustache who often had a faraway look in his eyes, as if he were looking past today and into tomorrow. He was a heavy smoker and his voice was very deep and very loud. He walked with wonky legs that seemed to have minds of their own.

The other doubler seller was a tall, lugubrious man who worked as an undertaker. He committed suicide in the end.

Both of these men – the soothsaying cripple and the doomed undertaker – would wander up and down the sidelines with leather pouches in front of them selling tickets for the first point scorers. It was a harmless form of gambling that I never quite understood. You'd purchase a ticket and receive two numbers that corresponded to the players on the ground; if your numbered player scored you'd win. The two double sellers would bellow their cryptic creed as they weaved around the ground: 'Eight for ten, sixteen for twenty! Get your doubles eight for ten and sixteen for twenty!' I had no idea what they meant but their hypnotic chant would mingle with the sound from the queue for the beer tent...

'Eight for ten!'

'What ya want?'

'No flavoured milk here!'

'Sixteen for twenty!'

'Sorry. Jesus, sorry.'

'Mind your cigarette!'

'Come on, come on, what ya want?'

'Try the ladies auxiliary. Was that Tony?'

'Who scored?'

'No flavoured milk. Where's me Escorts?'

'Eight for ten...'

'I'll bloody hit you in a minute. There's no flavoured milk!'

'Sixteen for twenty!'

There was a man in front of me in the queue wearing a blue-and-white striped shirt with the collar turned up, and caramel polyester shorts with a large studded black belt threaded through the loops. His thonged feet flopped in turn. What mesmerised me most, though, was the length of his arms. He looked like a character from a Dr Seuss story. He clenched a cigarette in his right hand and the cigarette hung almost to his ankles. He'd fling it slowly up to his mouth to take a drag, but rather than lift his hand he'd swing his long arm like a pendulum in bigger arcs until with a final heave he'd rush the fag to his mouth, suck it with a hiss and then let his hand fall back. As it fell he would straighten his elbow, and his hand, with the burning cigarette, would swing back and out along its long trajectory... Right towards my face. It came so close I could see the melting strands of tobacco and the emblem on the thin paper: Escort. His swinging limb kept time with his flapping feet and through it all intoned the metronomic call of the double sellers.

'Eight for ten.'

Swing, suck, flap the feet, sixteen for twenty, let the arm fall, the baccy burns...

By the time I reached the front of the queue I was close to zombie status, hypnotised by the rhythms around me. But then the striped shirt and the caramel pants and the thonged feet and the swinging arm disappeared and I stared ahead and saw an uncurling hand with a gently flapping finger. I looked up and there was a man staring off after the bloke in the striped shirt.

'That bugger has arms like an oranga-fucking-tan.'

From the other side of the beer tent someone answered, 'He comes from Kippa-Ring. He's a panel beater.'

'I don't care,' said the man with the gently flapping finger. 'He's got arms like an oranga-fucking-tan.' He looked down at me. 'What ya want, chief?'

I didn't say a thing.

He looked at me and said again, 'What ya want, chief, what ya want?'

From somewhere far, far away, came my voice; I tried to yell like everyone else but I ended up sounding like a halfwit. 'Arseholes and lips!'

'Eight for ten, sixteen for twenty!' cried the double seller.

The man with the gently flapping finger lurched forward. His digit flicked back and forth, like the fingers of actors in kung-fu movies, inviting further battle. 'What *ya* want? What *ya* want?'

'Three hotdogs and a Tarax please.' Now I just sounded gormless.

From a steaming silver box emerged the hotdogs. I could see them swimming in oily water. The can of Tarax was cold. As I turned away the man with the gently flapping finger said to someone in the beer tent, 'Jesus, where do these buggers come from?' Was he talking about me or the hotdogs?

The hotdog tasted like cardboard and it was cold in the middle. I threw it away and ate the bun.

'Bevan's playing!' someone screamed.

Bevan Bleakley was a legend, deadset, no argument – tough as nails and as hard as rocks; a hatchet-faced redhead with sideburns and a rocker's haircut. Merv Cook was a legend too – a winger with a pencil-thin moustache and a scuttling run that resembled a drunken crab. So too Bunny Pearce, an ambling fullback from the high country who laughed when one of his mongrel kicks for goal somehow made its way between the posts.

They were all part of a motley crew that were the mighty Redcliffe Dolphins; a rugby league team that played in the Brisbane competition in the seventies in the days before the NRL, the Broncos and even State of Origin; the days when the big game in Brisbane was suburb against suburb.

Dad loved going to the rugby league, mainly, I think, to yell and scream; never nastily, mind you. I loved going with him. He would yell at the most inappropriate times and yell things that quite often had absolutely no connection with the game. He would get the players' names wrong and his ubiquitous 'characters' abounded in every team: Hughie O'Doherty, the bald-headed hooker from the Valley Die-hards who stole the ball in tackles with the driven passion of a psychotic kleptomaniac. Howard Fullerton, a fullback from Easts who could kick a goal from sixty metres and could run about ten centimetres; and the accurately named Chips 'Half-a-game' Harrington from Brothers who had superior ball skills but was a shot duck by the forty-minute mark.

Even those on the sidelines seemed larger than life. George Doniger and Mick Veivers were two of the best footy callers I have ever heard. They were accurate, passionate and would rabbit on like best mates. George's catchcry was, 'Oh you beauty!' and his immortal 'That's champagne football, that is!' Apparently Mick went into politics. But the most colossal caller was a bloke named Fonda Metassa, the Golden Greek. Fonda was a caller on 4BH and had a style that made Darrell Eastlake look like Marcel Marceau. To say he was loud was an understatement. I saw him once at Lang Park screaming from his box, while next door a journalist was banging on the wall with all his might yelling, 'For Christ's sake, shut up!' Fonda's great claim to fame was the night he got the hiccups in the middle of calling a game. Truly one of the great digestive affected moments of football broadcasting. His hiccups sounded like the noise the neighbour's dog, Penny, made when she got run over by the baker one morning. Lots of screeching and howling. As Fonda himself would say (sorry, shriek), 'What a doozy!'

The Dolphins scooped the pool when it came to larger-than-life characters. It all started for me in 1973 when a waspish-tongued former halfback named Barry Muir was the coach. As a stylist Barry wasn't much to look at, even though he'd played for Australia his biggest achievement was once gobbing at a ref. But as a motivator he had no equal and he could make paint peel from the walls and his players run right through them. And then there was Merv Cook and Bevan

Bleakley. Merv copped a lot of flack in our house, always getting the blame for any loss or poor performance.

'Merv bleeding bloody Cook,' Dad would growl. Mum would try to stand up for Merv, as if he were some slightly feeble and simple-minded member of the family. But my father would have none of it. 'Why do they play that man? Why?' he'd ask each of us in turn. Even the dog.

But not on one particular day at the Redcliffe showgrounds. Playing for a spot in the finals for the first time in years, Redcliffe was up against the Wests Panthers, a team that boasted three internationals. The odds weren't great. Wests attacked the Redcliffe line and spun the ball through their slick backs.

'Oh, here we go, here we bloody go,' growled my father as Merv jiggled about on his wing. It seemed inevitable they would score until Merv took destiny and the ball in his hands. Merv the panicked crab had snared the intercept and ran and ran and ran. And as he ran a roar from the crowd seemed to curl with a great surge behind him and Merv rode it like a wave. He was chased by three of the fastest men in the comp but somehow he managed to outrun them, and when Warren Oar, an international winger, lined Merv up for the tackle and dived towards him, from somewhere deep in his past Merv summoned a fend to Oar's head and palmed the flashy player away.

The showgrounds erupted. Articles of clothing, hotdogs, car keys and cans of drink were thrown into the air. Adults hugged each other and Dad, like so many others, could do no more than bellow with delight, 'Merv Cook! Merv Cook! Merv bleeding bloody Cook!'

I clapped until my hands were numb.

On that day, at the age of ten, when I saw so many people so happy, I thought just about anything was possible.

Merv walked back along the sideline breathing hard with his hands on his hips and his head lowered. Despite the cheers and the adulation, he didn't look towards the noise. In his moment of triumph, his humility and modesty made what he'd done even more epic. There was no showboating from Merv; he looked almost embarrassed with the attention.

As he walked past me I was so moved I had to say something. 'Well played, Merv Cook!' Whether there was a break in the noise, or perhaps I yelled louder than I meant to, I don't know but I said it and Merv Cook heard me and looked up. He looked me square in the eyes for a few moments and as he passed he gave a small nod in acknowledgment and then carried on his way back to his position deep in the corner of the ground.

Two of Bevan Bleakley's finest moments occurred at Lang Park. One was during a match against Brothers. The Redcliffe halfback Brian Winney had exchanged pleasantries with Chips 'Half-a-Game' Harrington and lay comatose on the turf. As Chips ambled back into line, I don't think he saw Bevan. I certainly hope he didn't. Being hit by a truck is bad, to see it coming just adds to the horror. Before anyone knew what was going on, a flaming redhead crashed into Chips, and when the dust settled, Half-a-Game lay belly up to the sun, his heaving butcher-striped Brothers' jersey signifying that not even half a game would be played that day. The roar from the outer was deafening and the smell of half-digested Chiko Rolls wafted across the ground as Bevan strode around the arena.

Bevan's other defining moment came in the immortal 1975 Grand Final against Wests. Wests were pasting Redcliffe; slaughtering them in fact, and Barry Muir must have raised hell and lowered heaven in his halftime address because the Dolphins came out steaming. Bevan Bleakley played like a cyclone and, resembling a cross-between a Jackie Chan kung-fu movie and an earthquake, he ran through half the forward pack and the backline to score a sensational try in the corner. Bleakley karate-chopped and bounced the Wests players left, right and centre and went on to carry another three over the line. When he stood, he left them lying at his feet.

Redcliffe never won a Grand Final, but they always found great ways to lose them. In spite of this the town never tired of them, and I can recall following them to the other hot spots around Brisbane: Neumann Oval, Corbett Park, Purtell Park and Davies Park.

During one game at Davies Park there was a man in front of us who'd been moaning ever since kick-off. He'd complained about the referee, the weather, his wife, his children and his team. He'd clearly had enough. He stomped off to buy a Chiko Roll, which in those days were always served cold, or lukewarm if you were lucky. Sure enough, after ten minutes or so, Mr Moaner came back and had a whine about the queue at the stall. Then he flapped his arms and went berserk. They hadn't given him his Chiko Roll – he'd paid for it and they'd bloody well ripped him off! He kept moaning until he sat down, completely forgetting that he'd put the thing in his pocket. As luck would have it, it was one of the few scorching Chikos ever sold, and just before his bum hit the bench I noticed steam pouring from his rear. Amid the cries of the crowd came an exquisite roar of pain and anguish. 'My Chiko! My Fuck…ing Chiko Roll! My Chiko Fuck…ing Roll!' Even the players turned and stared.

The action seemed closer back then; you could smell the liniment on the players, hear them call their moves, hear the oaths and the struggles. It was a different Brisbane; a little rougher maybe, certainly more of a small town, but a town that was richer in the way its people interacted. Every suburb had its own character, its own politic; and its footy competition was a way in which those traits were played out. The players weren't million-dollar men, just ordinary blokes down the road who happened to play footy on the weekends.

Bunny Pearce, the buzz-cut hick from the high country whose laugh you could hear from the sidelines and who was one of those rare men who nobody could ever say a bad word about, died not so long ago in a car accident. When I heard, I felt such a sadness; a sorrow that seems odd because I never even said boo to Bunny Pearce. But I knew him and I remembered the joy that he and the other players had given me. I went to my study just to sit, and without really even thinking found my old autograph book from 1973. The finals team had assembled at Woolies in Margate on the Saturday before the big game, and they stood around the aisles of food signing autographs and meeting fans. I was able to get Bevan

Bleakley's autograph – he was leaning against the frozen food section staring into its icy depths. I could hardly bring myself to speak as I proffered my autograph book. I poked him with my pen. As one of the fiercest men in league scribbled his name he stared into the fridge and whispered, 'Jesus, them fish fingers are cheap.'

These were the only words I ever heard Bevan Bleakley speak.

The real estate man made-good speaks off the cuff in fits and starts, as if he's holding an auction. He reminds me of an Australian version of the American film actor Christopher Walken.

'Friends...friends...friends...friendsfriendsfriendsfriends, it's good to see so many friends.'

He speaks about the old days, when Redcliffe was a collection of small farms and not much else. He tells stories of how he acquired property – sitting beside a farmer who didn't want to sell and hand-milking the cows every day for a week. Constantly bargaining and milking. Then another week, until at last the farmer sold his land and that land was then used for more 'appropriate development'. Appropriate development becomes the recurring theme of the real estate man-made good's speech: Redcliffe had undergone a property boom and everywhere you looked new estates and high-rise developments were appearing. It was the main industry these days. But they hadn't forgotten the past; there were monuments to early European explorers such as Oxley and Flinders, and streets and avenues and parks and reserves named after them.

Monuments to the earlier inhabitants are harder to find.

I went for a walk around a new 'unique blue-water development' estate that had been given an Aboriginal-sounding name. It meant 'Wild Dolphin', or at least that's what the sign said. A real estate salesman I knew from school had showed me around and I asked him if it were true. He looked up at the sign and smiled. 'Yeah well, maybe. But I can tell you this for nothing, it's Abo for making me a shitload of money.'

Appropriate development indeed.

The real estate man made-good went on to talk about the tasty rolls that the bakery on Oxley Avenue used to sell. 'Oh they were good...good...good...goodgoodgood...good goodgood. Soft and white... White and soft. But it was a bad space, so I bought and sold that bakery for a more appropriate development. It's a car yard now. And there's so much more...more land and space...space that's ripe for appropriate development.'

A woman in a nice suit at a nearby table whispered to the man sitting next her, 'Space like the showgrounds.' She waved her arm in a circle. 'Everyone loves a show.'

'But for *three* days of the year?' said her friend, letting the question hang in the air. She was still tracing the arc of the ferris wheel.

In fact the show had just finished and for the first time in years I'd gone. I'd taken my son. He loves shows.

As a young boy I'd walk up a partially sealed road past the trotting track, over Humpybong Creek, across Crash Corner, past the dark sawmill that always smelt of shaved wood and made me think of my father, and finally onto the showgrounds.

Nowadays Oxley Avenue has four sealed lanes and the old sawmill has been replaced by the icons of suburbia – a Sizzlers, a McDonald's, an all-night service station and a video store. The showgrounds are still there, however, surrounded by a cocoon of tall spotted gum trees. Walking along the fence I remember several of my attempts to gain access to the show without paying; a sort of *Great Escape* in reverse. A few times I made it over the barbed wire, but more often than not the vaguely medical-looking stewards in white coats would heave me back the way I'd come. One lunatic attempt with my neighbor Reggie Worth had been inspired by a physical education class the previous day. Optimistically, we had attempted to high-jump the fence using the scissors method and were lucky not to castrate ourselves as we leapt, with flailing teenage frames, kamikaze-like at the barbed wire.

I resisted the temptation to repeat my efforts and instead wandered through the turnstiles. When the children of the Peninsula were given the Friday off school for the show, it gave us an importance that set us apart from the rest of the state. It made the Redcliffe Peninsula special. These days the show is held during the last week of the regular school holidays, and I wondered if the kids on the Peninsula looked forward to it as much as I had.

'The kids have got so much more to do these days,' said the woman at the turnstiles. 'There's that MovieWorld thingy down the coast, and Brisbane just up the road. It's not what it was – but it's still our little show. Six dollars, thanks.'

Six dollars? I thought about high-jumping the fence but decided against it and paid up. As I walked through the caravans of sideshow alley, I heard the echoes of the Holden Precision Driving Team: heroes of shows past. Four men in different coloured Monaros hooning around the centre ring, charging at each other at full tilt, missing by centimetres and eliciting screams of terror and delight from the audience. It had made such an impact on us that we had tried to emulate the boys in the Holden Precision Driving Team down at the Woolies car park, using shopping trolleys instead of V8 Monaros. I still sport a scar on the back of my knee where our precision trolley driving went astray.

The sideshow alley hadn't changed all that much – there were still men on the dodgems, leaping from car to car, looking tough and lean in flannelette shirts and black jeans. The laughing clowns, the shooting gallery, the haunted house. I went into the haunted house once and felt ripped off because the hairy ghoul at the second bend was Tony Grimshaw, one of my classmates at Humpybong Primary. I felt like asking for my money back. This year's show had a haunted house that promised 'genuine terror in scare-conditioned comfort'. It looked very small and I wondered if its budget ran to a hairy ghoul at the second bend. The shooting gallery proclaiming 'Life's fun with a gun' looked somewhat chilling with the battered yellow ducks clanking above the array of stuffed toys, which were prizes for good marksmanship.

It was all a bit forlorn and sad. The vendors were half-heartedly trying to entice some custom. 'She'll be right when there's a few more people here, mate. Then things'll crank up,' said Percy, who ran the hammer of strength stall. 'Have a go and test your strength!'

I had a go, hit the bell at the top and won the 'mug's prize', a plastic dummy. Percy smiled and gave me a wink, 'It's a game of skill as well as strength, matey, just like life.'

Sideshow alley psychology classes.

The rides whirled around half-filled with screaming people and music blaring distortedly from old speakers. Some of the rides were familiar and had names like racehorses or wrestlers: the Hurricane, the Octopus, the Gravitron and the immortal Tilt-a-Whirl. Immortal in my family. I went on it once with my Aunty Rita and sister Corby, and it was an experience none of us has ever forgotten. It was a small cabin that spins around quickly and at great force. Aunty Rita had the idea to go on a ride after we had all just eaten a hamburger and slurped down a milkshake. I have never officially re-entered the earth's atmosphere or had an out-of-body experience, but the Tilt-a-Whirl with a stomach chock-full of junk food combined with a screaming sister and a cackling aunty loudly proclaiming, 'I'm going to peeeeeee! I have to PeeeeEEEEEEEE!' is the next best thing. I had been sandwiched into the end of the cabin as we all wheezed, screamed and cackled with terror and delirium.

One time on the ferris wheel, I saw a girl in my class whom I was sure I loved and I knew would love me if only I'd have had the courage to tell her or even managed to pass on an intelligible word. She was kissing a boy two grades my senior.

I stared as he held her in his arms and the wheel scooped them up into the night sky and out of my heart. I stumbled away and the lights from the fast food stalls and rides shone into my face, highlighting my tortured teenaged blush. The speakers blared, loud and distorted, but the song that played as I stole another look at the ferris wheel up in the stars was: 'The Monster Mash'.

I'm hungry. The spruikers call just as they used to, imploring passers-by to taste the delights of the Dagwood Dog: a saveloy sausage encased in bullet-proof batter, deep-fried and dripping with tomato sauce. Skewered with a stick they look more like some medieval weapon of war than something you'd try to digest. So I drift away. The crowds seemed thinner than I remembered and although the local Lions Club had a food stall there was no giant lucky wheel and, alas, no Swimming Club hamburgers. My brother and I ate thousands of those wonderful creations and I still haven't found a burger to equal them anywhere in my travels. Mum said it was because one of the local butchers' sons was in the club so the stall received extra special mince that hadn't been 'fiddled with'. Crowned with lightly fried onions, nestling in fresh lettuce and tomato and then covered with Mrs Cusack's special sauce, the burgers were superb. The quality was summed up nicely by Uncle Reg, who proclaimed after a trip to the RSL with Dad that he'd 'Take me teeth out and dance naked on the Pope's bed', if he ever found a better burger. Thankfully for Uncle Reg and the Holy Father, he never found one.

The show's woodchoppers were as exciting as ever and I cheered along with everyone else as the back marker caught up his handicap and went on to win, attacking the wood just like my mother used to attack the iced-over freezer, sending chips flying about the room in record time.

The food hall was healthy enough with novelty cakes (my favourite being a cake moulded into the form of a cement mixer) and pikelets, scones and odd-looking loaves of bread. Preserved fruit in tall glass jars looked like bottled rainbows. Most of the jars were old Pablo coffee containers, ones like my nanna used to buy. It struck me that Nanna had been dead for almost thirty years and that whoever had entered these exhibits had been doing so for a long, long time. Maybe these jars had been entered by a woman like my nanna? Year after year come showtime she would clean out her old Pablo coffee jars and preserve her coloured fruits, shuffling about and singing softly under her breath while her grandchildren scurried under her feet.

Most of the paintings in the art section were competent and depicted the local area, but a few were dreadful in that wonderful way only local art competitions can be; my favourite being the giant Christ figure wandering across Moreton Bay towards Woody Point with a flock of seagulls flying around him.

'He wants to be careful they don't shit on him,' an old man mumbled to his friend as he viewed the Messiah and his flock.

When I wandered into the Tommy Atkinson Hall to view the school artwork, I felt the rush of excitement I had felt all the times I had raced in expectantly to see if my pieces had received awards. Not surprisingly I usually lucked out with my barely recognisable sconecutters and cheeseboards made during the tortuous manual training classes. The only time I tasted success was when I made a plaster-of-Paris battle scene that I'd copied from a *Commando* war comic. But the hall today was brimming with the most brilliant colours and creations. Surrounded by multi-coloured sea monsters and essays of 'My City Redcliffe', this part of the show seemed vibrant and alive. A young girl of about twelve let out a whoop of joy and ran to her father.

'I won, I won, I won at the show!' she cried, beaming and dragging her father to a painting of fireworks exploding over a trawler.

Fireworks were always the last great event at the show, and for years it was blessed with a ring announcer with the most extraordinary voice. It was English, a Berkshire drawl, and it sounded as if it belonged to Long John Silver. 'Now boys an' girrrrrrrls. Would ye liiiiiiike the firrrrrreworrrrrrks?' While the flares exploded above the crowd Long John Silver growled. 'Arrrr, they look liiiiiike spiderrrrrrs in the sky!'

As the new ring announcer called for the fireworks I sensed that the show was no longer such an important event and that perhaps the woman at the gate had been right about the kids having so much to do these days. I held my son up in my arms and we watched the spectacular display in the sky. It struck me that I had been held the same way by my mother and father when I was my son's age. I looked around and saw some people who I had been to school with and they too were holding their children up. One in particular caught my attention; the last time I had seen her was on the ferris wheel and 'Monster Mash' had been playing. At that moment a particularly brilliant flare exploded and as one the crowd sighed. The fireworks drifted across the night sky and I remembered my youth and Long John Silver. I held my son close and pointed upwards, 'Arrr, they look like spiders in the sky.'

My son looked towards the heavens and shouted with delight.

9

The annual show didn't have a monopoly on the grounds. Not only was it the home of the football and hockey clubs, it was also the home of various 'cultural pursuits'. The amateur theatrical society was one of the most prominent and was housed in the old rugby clubhouse. The theatre was very small but the shows the society performed were huge. It was like staging a production of *Camelot* and the Battle of Agincourt performed with music in your garden shed. Some of the performers were well-known – the bloke from the hardware shop and the fellow from the real estate office down by the jetty who blinked a lot. And there was the milkman who, as Mum said, 'Was a bit touched.' When he spoke he always seemed to be engaged in a prolonged yawn; when he sang it was even more noticeable. He was usually in the chorus but would inevitably become the centre of attention because it's hard to miss the person who sings on long after everyone else has stopped.

The amateur theatrical society did in fact stage *Camelot* as well as other classics such as *Desert Song*. For the knights in *Camelot* a local welding works had pitched in and made the armour. It was very impressive and very heavy. As the theatre was so small, when King Arthur and his friends danced and jousted, the floor and the seats would tremble and shake. 'Jesus wept,' my father whispered as softly as he could. He still ended up sounding like a sergeant major on a parade ground. My brother said it was like 'sensoround' – the sound system that cinemas in the seventies installed to give added atmosphere to disaster movies. You could feel the cinema move under your feet. At the old rugby clubhouse everything from the floor to false teeth moved and when Lancelot came on bits and pieces of ceiling rained down on the stage. He was very large and very loud. And his arms! Those arms again. I knew those arms. The beer tent queue at the football, the burning Escort pendulating back and forth. Only this time he wasn't wearing a striped shirt and thongs. He was in the heaviest piece of metal worn since Ned Kelly of Glenrowan. Even beneath his wrought iron I recognised him. I smelt hotdogs. 'Arseholes and lips,' I said when I saw him.

My mother gave me a clip and my father said, 'Jesus Christ Almighty, watch your bloody mouth. You leave that language in the dairy.'

I tried to explain. 'I know that guy...he was at the football and –' I was cut off by a low rumbling that grew to a terrific noise. Lancelot, my long-armed friend from the hotdog queue, was singing.

'Dear me, he sounds like a cyclone warning,' said a woman behind us. When he sang he'd ball his heavily gloved hands into fists the size of bowling balls and when he sang 'C'est Moi' he pointed into the distance, and his arms seemed to reach out over the heads of the audience and right to the back wall of the theatre. People ducked their heads. King Arthur was an odd counterpoint to the looming Lancelot. He was as bald as a badger and slightly trembly in his heavy armour. When he sang, his vibrato was extenuated by the clanking iron, especially as he was determined to stand on his toes every time Lancelot was around.

My father looked at King Arthur with narrowed eyes. 'Jesus Christ, he looks like Billy bloody McMahon.' These comments would have been fine if he'd uttered them *sotto voce*, but when Dad spoke they came out like the exclamation of some mad scientist. Everybody in the theatre heard him of course, including all those on stage. King Arthur/Billy McMahon turned to the audience, ostensibly to deliver an icy stare, but as he swivelled, a bit of his costume gave way under the strain and part of his armour fell off. It was the lower half. Without a counter weight to hold everything in place the front top half sprung to attention and it looked to my young eyes as though King Arthur/Billy McMahon had cracked a massive fat. I don't think I was the only one to have this thought as there was a gasp from the audience, and when King Arthur/Billy McMahon grandly launched into his mighty vibrato to 'Bring me Lancelot, I am ready for this Noble Knight,' the gasps turned to guffaws.

Desert Song was about Arabs. And beards. Everyone seemed to have beards, even the women. One memorable performance, during a torrid love scene in the Red Shadow's boudoir – he was the only person not to have a beard, by the way, but he did have an enormous lisp, it took me a moment to realise 'thord', 'thccratch' and 'thkin' was actually 'sword', 'scratch' and 'skin' – the walls collapsed. Thankfully they were caught by a man with a beard. He wasn't supposed to be there, he was just a beard dressed as an Arab helping out. The love scene progressed and the prop wall was slowly inched upright. 'Watch out, Reg!' came a cry and Reg did a double-take when he saw another prop wall falling. Right on top of him. His beard was squashed flat. Across his face. He looked like a singing toilet brush.

Aside from the delights of the local thespian productions, the showground oval hosted numerous 'artistic events'. One unforgettable troupe was the French–Canadian Hell Drivers. These were a group of stunt drivers who would chew up the oval and the football ground in their hotted-up old HQ Holdens and Vauxhalls. They were led by the exotic sounding Josey Kanga. This was a big event, they even had advertisements on the television. We fell off our chairs when Telly showed us that Redcliffe was the destination of Josey and his French–Canadian driving friends. Josey had long hair and sideburns that looked like he'd borrowed them from someone from the amateur theatrical society's production of *Maid of the Mountains*. In the ad, Josey was dressed in his racing jumpsuit but he had dispensed with his helmet. He had his arms around two girls in bikinis. He smiled. He had more bits of teeth missing than a second-hand jigsaw puzzle. The voiceover man said, 'That Josey may not speak much English but he sure loves Australian girls.'

'INTERNATIONAL ENTERTAINMENT COMES TO THE REDCLIFFE PENINSULA' screamed the headline in the *Redcliffe Herald*, accompanied by a photo of a winking Josey (without the girls in bikinis this time). Dad read the paper in his 'Chair' which sat in the corner by the stove. 'French–Canadian Hell Drivers,' he said, almost to himself. The stove was having a bad day and as it belched wisps of smoke, Dad was enveloped in an atmospheric fog. 'French–Canadian Hell Drivers,' he said again. He got up and proceeded to walk around the house muttering to himself. His imagination had obviously been sparked. Later, when we were having dinner, he chewed mightily on a piece of meat and then as casually as he could he mentioned that, 'It might be an idea if we went and had a gander at these blokes up the showgrounds.' Nobody was quite sure who he was talking about. 'They're tough buggers, you know, most of them could be fur trappers or lumberjacks.'

'What are you talking about, Colin?' Mum asked in her most polite voice.

My father stared at us as if surrounded by idiots. 'They cut bloody trees down, these blokes.' And he pointed a knife towards the light fitting. 'These French–Canadian blokes.'

The showgrounds were packed on the Sunday afternoon the Hell Drivers brought their special form of entertainment to Redcliffe. Looking back, I realise Redcliffe had always had a deep appreciation of motor sport. It was not unknown for us to be lolling about on a weekend only to have the peace and quiet disturbed by screeching brakes and the sound of metal meeting metal. 'Merry Christmas,' Dad would say, and we'd be off; running through the prickles towards Crash Corner – the intersection of Oxley and Anzac avenues. We weren't the only ones. Small crowds would gather to check out the accidents. In fact it was such a ritual that Crash Corner became a part of almost everybody's weekend.

One Monday morning at show and tell a boy called Ian Taylor presented a piece of twisted metal, saying it was from an accident at Crash Corner. I knew he was lying because there hadn't been any screeching, my father hadn't said 'Merry Christmas' and we definitely hadn't run through the prickles. But I didn't say anything. Why ruin someone's show and tell?

One boy, a tough kid who used to trick dive off the jetty in cut-off jeans and spit at us younger boys, was sitting in a purple Cortina one afternoon at Crash Corner. The front was crumpled in and he was sobbing and snot was dribbling from his nose. He was rolling up the windows. His father was banging on what was left of the bonnet and screaming at his blubbing son to get out of the car.

His son shook his head. 'You'll hit me,' he moaned.

Dad appeared out of nowhere and his big hand fell gently on my head and he took me home. Later, they installed traffic lights at that intersection and people soon stopped calling it

Crash Corner. Out on the jetty nobody paid much attention to the tough's trick dives either.

So we were all primed for the French–Canadian Hell Drivers. They had one particularly surreal trick where Josey Kanga drove an old EH Holden up a ramp, through the goal posts and onto a line of old bombs. There'd be a huge crash and out through the battered window would crawl a groggy-looking Josey in a very saggy jumpsuit. His arm was wobbly when he waved, but he still managed to do it with great flair.

My father turned to Uncle Reg. 'Tip-top show this.'

Uncle Reg nodded. 'Top shelf, Col. Don't see this every day.'

It was true. It's not every day you see an old EH Holden arc through a set of goal posts. I had a camera, one with an ice-cube flash, which I barely knew how to use, but somehow I managed to catch this moment on film. It was a marvellous day; it had everything, even a television camera crew who stood on top of the old scoreboard that was a regular source of embarrassment for the footy fans. It was a small square structure with long prongs of steel that held up the numbers. I was desperate to get on camera but I refrained from jumping up or making faces to get my head on Telly. I took a more low-key approach; I was a keen photographer after all, going about my business, checking my state-of-the-art instamatic with its high-tech ice-cube flash. Back and forth I tottered. The cameraman perched on the scoreboard swore under his breath. I quickened my pace and before I knew it somehow smacked my head into one of the steel prongs. I shrieked and clicked the camera and caught Josey's magic moment. I was rushed off by my father who stuck my head under a tap and soothingly told me that there was nothing wrong with an egg on your scone. When I cried a bit he took me to the beer tent and bought me a ginger beer.

For years afterwards, when he would drive his truck with his homemade tables and trestles, my father would toot his horn at anyone he thought was driving in a dangerous or ineffective manner and wave with both hands hanging from the cab, yelling, 'Hey, you bloody stupid Josey Kanga,' or more iconically 'French–Canadian Hell Driver Bastard.' I remember driving along Macdonald Road with my father going on about Merv bloody Cook and him nearly being collected by a ute driven by Megsy Bainbridge. They both laughed uproariously. 'You might not speak much English,' yelled my father.

'But I sure like Australian girls,' screamed back Megsy.

I wonder what happened to Josey Kanga. Being a French–Canadian Hell Driver didn't seem to be a long-term occupation. Maybe he still plied his trade in creaking old bombs around the world with that brave little wave to indicate he was still in one piece and up for more mayhem. Wherever he was he wasn't here in the swankiest restaurant in town.

The real estate man made-good was warming to his subject. It was wonderful, he said, how much the shops in Redcliffe had changed. How 'the shops...the stores. *Yesyesyes Yes!* The outlets! Had changed. Appropriate Development!'

I thought of the shops that sat atop Marine Parade. They were either crazy bargain junk stores, pawn shops or chemists that sold a lot of Zimmer frames and incontinence pads.

When I was a boy, I'd go to the haberdashery department of a shop called Barry and Roberts. It sounds like a dinner party at a gay couple's house. Barry and Robert's, the happy bachelors. Where everything matches and is always clean.

Every Friday afternoon around four-thirty Mum would go to the haberdashery department and pick material and patterns to make clothes. She'd always smile and say to the woman behind the counter, 'This time I'll get it right, the last one wasn't too bad, she only looked like half a hunchback.' She was talking about my sister's new dress. And she would laugh, and the woman behind the counter would laugh.

Once we saw a beautiful purple fabric. It was so lovely it shone, and it was so soft. It floated down onto the counter, just before it was cut, like a soft breath. Mum bought a short length, just because it was so fine. She never did anything with it, but kept it wrapped in the green and white paper of Barry and Roberts, high in her cupboard of good things.

Barry and Roberts isn't there anymore, gone the way of ever more appropriate development. After Barry and Roberts vacated the building it became an army disposals store – two floors of junk the various countries' armies and navys didn't want anymore. It was almost like a museum. One year they had lots of old German and American helmets for sale at bargain prices. That summer outmoded army helmets came into fashion and you'd see people fishing out on the pier, or working in

161

the garden with small green foldout army spades wearing these helmets. Schoolkids in their uniforms walked to school with a German helmet on their heads.

Walking to the beach with Dad and Uncle Reg one afternoon, we passed a man mowing his lawn wearing thongs, one white sock, caramel shorts and a shirt with submarines and bathyspheres printed on it. He was smoking and was wearing dark sunglasses. And on top of his head was a German army helmet. As we walked by he yelled in answer to some unheard order, 'I'll do the fucking banana trees in a minute!'

My father spoke without looking at Uncle Reg. 'He's had a good Christmas.'

Uncle Reg replied without looking at my father. 'The last bloke I saw wearing a hat like that was through the sights of me rifle. Now the bloody milkman wears one… How'd we win the bloody war?'

Even better than the army helmet season was the summer of 1985 – the year of Shehu Shagari. I was home from uni and it was my job to buy the caps for the uni cricket team. Where else to go for cheap headwear but the army disposals store? There I found a box of baseball caps emblazoned with the bold texta message, 'Adjustable Size.' I opened the box to find sky-blue caps with a photographic image of a man dressed in African robes smiling beatifically on a great cane chair. He had sunglasses on and above him was written, 'Shehu Shagari. One Nation One Destiny'!

It looked like one of the bad records my sister used to own.

I bought the box and that summer we wore those caps playing baseball and cricket. Our team cry became, 'Shehu Shagari! One Nation One Destiny!' A little later I found out he was a former President of Nigeria. The caps were a part of his election campaign and were an attempt to bring his people together. Where did it all lead to? The army disposals store in Redcliffe, Queensland.

I remembered that and had another drink. Somehow the caps didn't seem so funny. A man's belief, a nation's hope and drunken boys in the Queensland sun.

With every word that the real estate man spoke, I had the feeling that the town where I grew up wasn't going to be the same for much longer. Is any place? What did it matter?

He was happy. 'This is a beautiful beautiful...beautiful place to be...to live...to do business. Our council are in... returned...a council who'll listen. It's great.' The local council had just been returned unopposed. And it was almost entirely made up of real estate agents. The man worked himself into a frenzy, '...and we'll have high rise. High rise, high rise, so more people can come and enjoy the beauty. It's all about Appropriate Development!'

He received a standing ovation. The sound made me think of rain on a tin roof. I remembered kissing a girl down on the beach under a roof of tin, smelling the salt in the air and her perfume. I wondered where she was and whether she still lived here in this town ripe for Appropriate Development. It wasn't much of a kiss really, as kisses go. Probably all teeth and a little too anxious, but a kiss on the beach is a kiss on the beach.

She was a year older than me and caught the same bus home from school. She'd get off a few stops before me and one day I thought to myself a walk on the beach would be nice. So I got off at her stop. As I walked down towards the beach, she walked on the other side of the street in the same direction. She walked right past her house and kept going. I knew it was her house because my father had delivered trestles to the house next door. I had helped him; it was Dad's plan to spend more time with me even though it was obvious he really didn't need any help (and probably didn't want any). So I stood around while he tried to be fatherly.

'For Christ's sake! Can you push that thing there?' I had no idea what he was talking about. He lurched off down the side of the house with his great heap of steel. So I leant against the back of the truck as he lunged and crashed in the backyard and I looked next door at the house and its front yard with two swans cut out of old car tyres standing either side of a green concrete path. The swans had some big flowers in pots placed between the wings, and a little hairy dog was dropping a poo just nearby. Somewhere a man was trying to start a mower. I looked at the little dog straining as it did its business.

The girl from the bus came down the stairs and picked up the straining dog.

'Come on, Dixie,' she said. Before she skipped back up the stairs, amazingly she smiled at me. 'Hello.'

'Hello,' I said back. The dog still looked as if it were straining. I hoped she hadn't picked Dixie up too soon. As my father heaved himself back into the truck and we drove slowly away, I heard someone scream. 'You filthy little thing!' Then came a yelp.

Dad looked at me. 'Bit of fun and games up there.'

'She picked up Dixie too soon,' I said.

My father stared at me and shook his head. 'Christ,' he muttered.

I thought that I should keep an eye on the girl on the bus who lived in the house with the car-tyre swans.

The girl on the bus and I left the swans behind and hit the beach at about the same time. A yellow council truck drove past and turned down into Suttons Beach as we waited to cross Marine Parade. The girl smiled at me and I tried to smile back. We walked across the road and onto the beach. We didn't say anything to each other. Rain started falling and we sat beneath a tin shelter on the beach.

'Wanna pash?' she said.

'Oh yeah, all right,' I replied.

And we snogged away while the rain fell and the council workers sat in the yellow truck and smoked and listened to the radio. I could just make out the tune; it was 'Put Another Log on the Fire' by a couple of singers called Bill and Boyd.

Our romance lasted for as long as the rain fell, which turned out to be only slightly longer than the song.

I saw her on the bus the next day and sat directly behind her. She didn't pay me any attention. As we neared her stop

I made one last impassioned plea to save our love. 'Hey, no chance of a bit of Bill and Boyding on the beach I suppose?'

She didn't bother to look at me. 'Get real.'

As she walked away, I pulled the window back and yelled, 'Put another log on the fire!'

Suttons Beach was the scene for many a jellyfish fight with Reg Worth. We favoured the sky-blue variety – the classic jellyfish. The fights were good fun. On one occasion, an English tourist asked us if the dark brown ones washed up on the beach were harmless. We assured him they were and he decided to pose in a novelty photo for 'the folks back 'ome'. He was bald and as white as a new bed sheet. He glowed in the sun. He wore togs that only a certain type of English person would ever wear – lime green and red tartan shorts with a white trim and a bit of string hanging from the belt. He also wore white socks and leather shoes. He organised his wife with the camera and smiled while he plopped the jellyfish on his bald head. As his wife snapped away, he began howling and within minutes his head looked like a relief map of some strange desert. A welt of red bumps stretched across his cranial landscape. Unfortunately I was in kicking distance.

Whenever I'm at the beach, any beach at all, I think of Dad. I used to dive off his big shoulders and have play fights, which miraculously I'd always win. I hear the waves and sometimes I can hear him laugh. Big and loud. I walked along the sand with him one night and asked the question that so many children ask their parents. 'What are the stars?'

He looked up and then looked back down to me. 'The stars,' he said, 'are holes in the sky that God made for the angels. God had to work pretty hard and when he went for a bit of a snooze the angels would peek down at night just to make sure we were all safe.'

I stood still for a moment, looking at all the glittering eyes of the angels and thought that was pretty good. Only one problem. The moon. What was the moon?

Without missing a beat, he replied, 'The moon? That's Jesus bending over.' After a moment of thought Dad whispered to me that it would be better if I didn't tell Mum that one.

One early evening as we walked along the beach, and looked across Moreton Bay and over to the islands, a huge electrical thunderstorm raged. The flashes of lightning glowed red-orange and the air was charged, the cavernous roll of thunder stopping us in our tracks. We stared. I was so excited. I held my father's hand tight.

'It's like a barrage,' he said. 'Laying down a barrage before they send you in. Poor bastards.' He stood on the beach with me but he was lost in another place and another time, with other people. Was he with his friends? Men he'd fought with in the war? Men he'd walked with as they had laid down a barrage? It made me realise that a whole section of his life was closed to me. I couldn't begin to imagine what he had seen and lived through. I held his hand tighter.

Sometimes on the beach I like to think I can feel it still.

When I studied drama in Perth there was a huge, quiet Islander woman who worked in the canteen. She would take our orders and timidly hand back our change or listen to excuses for why we had no money. There were times when she seemed so sad it was almost painful to talk to her and order lunch. The noise and confident banter of us boisterous, young students only made her plight seem worse.

I would go for runs along Perth's glorious beaches and, early one morning as I chugged along, I noticed one, lone person. It was a woman. A big woman. From where I ran on the bluff I don't think she could see me. I looked down. She was running from the water, or rather she was dancing from the water; skipping and dancing from the surf. Smiling. She stopped and turned back to the waves and with arms outstretched began to sing. She had the most beautiful voice and she sang a song of pure joy in a language I didn't understand. I didn't need to; on that beach, on that morning, I stood and listened to the sound of happiness.

I ran on, but I didn't forget that moment. Nor the moment at the canteen when as I ordered my food, I asked the big woman behind the counter, 'You like the beach, don't you?'

She had her arm outstretched to accept my money, but she paused and looked at me, then the most beautiful smile crept across her face. 'Oh yes, it's a magical place.'

A magical place. But the magic was different for different people. For most of the people in the restaurant it was a case of *hey presto*! But instead of pulling a rabbit out of a hat, a developer would pull a high-rise unit out of an old weatherboard house or fibro shack. The houses along the beach were disappearing; a high-rise apartment tower called 'Baywatch' was being built on top of Suttons Beach. At night its name was lit by lights on the arm of the construction crane. But whether by chance or design some bulbs had blown and the first two letters were missing. Blazing out across the bayside night was the message 'y watch'.

The changes along the waterfront hadn't all been recent, but enough was happening to make it hard to remember what had once stood before. The *Gayundah*, Queensland's own naval flagship from colonial days, was beached on Woody Point to help prevent erosion. It's still there but each time I visit, a little more has been claimed by the elements. The old wreck is the colour of dark chocolate and like chocolate it seems to be slowly melting in the sun. The water is blue and the dark colours flake and sink into the Bay. There's something poetic about its demise. Something moving. You can see time passing; sense the hardness of the steel slowly losing its fight to exist.

Uncle Reg never quite understood why you would call a flagship the *Gayundah*. 'I know it's Aboriginal for something,' he said. 'But it really wasn't much of a name for a battleship.' It was hardly a battleship. And it may have had an odd sounding name, but Uncle Reg would never refer to it as the wreck. It was always the *Gayundah*. He would stand and look at her. Lots of people did. Older people.

When I was a little boy I saw a parade of soldier crabs scuttling across the decks. We laughed and chased the smartly coloured creatures back and forth, their blue shells glistening as they danced across the rust and deep brown of the *Gayundah*. The decks have gone now and I suppose from the top floors of the high-rise that stand on the bluff the *Gayundah* may well just look like bits of rock, bits of shell, bits of nothing.

Development and building are the boon industries on the Peninsula. They have been since the seventies and sometimes landmarks that vanish are replaced by another vision that seems to have been there forever. Settlement Cove is such a place. It's a man-made lagoon that was carved into the foreshore just below the shops. The water is pooled from the sea and then pumped back out again. There are picnic areas and tables and little grassy knolls made from synthetic substances on which people can recline and bake in the sun. Landscaped gardens surround the pools and the fronds of palm trees wave slowly in the breeze. It's in constant use, and the sound of children playing carries on just as loudly there as it did in the old days down on the beach. The lagoon looks more like Gilligan's Island than anything the first settlers may have encountered but happy sounds and fun only make historical appropriateness recede. My children love going to Gilligan's even though they've never seen the television show.

The Rollerdrome was an even more feverish bed of activity than the beach. It was built in the 1940s and was a square, flat piece of concrete that wasn't particularly fancy but was very effective. It was built right on the shorefront next to Anzac Park and although it had a roof its wired walls were open to the bay and the elements. It was almost medieval: you would enter through a front door and pay at a tiny window. A hand would appear and money would be exchanged. You would squeak out your shoe size and be given a leathery waxen pair of skates. There was almost no space to sit down; just a few benches on which to squat and lace yourself up before lurching off into the maelstrom of the rink.

Like so much of Redcliffe, it was past its use-by date when I was growing up. I got the arse end of these buildings, these places. But so strong was their character, so rich was the human experience that they had held, they seemed alive.

Music would blare out from speakers that indicated the type of skate session you were to be involved in. My skinny legs and awkward limbs would somehow manage to maintain a stuttering circle across the shiny concrete. The fine cracks showing like veins in a leg through grey stockings.

I moved contentedly through the ranks of novice juniors. I wasn't a great stylist but I had reached the point of looking awkward in a reasonably competent sort of way. Through the wire walls I could see the waters of the Bay stretching like a shimmering floor. It was quite lovely. I remember serenely rolling to the tune of 'Banks of the Ohio' sung by Olivia Newton-John. She sounded so funny with her English O's and her whiny good-girl pronunciation. It was a bizarre song about someone killing someone they loved by a river in America. Sung in a bland, weird, old-fashioned accent it was oddly numbing. Musical kava. I placidly moved on.

In fact, I quite dozed away as my skeletal frame rolled with the flow of mind-numbing musical drivel. I even joined in the chorus, sounding out my pure O's to match Olivia's. Until I found myself stranded. In the middle. Like a fool I let go of the safety of the wire and the walls and drifted innocently out into the middle. Out into the deep.

The blurred voice of the rink announcer cut across my doze. 'Speeeeeeeeeed Skateeeeerrrrs... Speeeeeeeed Skaaateeeers.'

A pounding in my chest mixed into the beat. I nearly wet myself. Deep Purple boomed 'Black Night'. All the toughs with weird mullets and bad tatts and broken teeth appeared in their tight jeans; their packets of fags squeezed in beneath their lurid body shirts. Big belt buckles and narrowed eyes. The slow swinging of their arms. I farted. For an awful moment I thought I'd shat myself. I stank. I heard a wheezy whine behind me. It was a fat boy called Doogles; he too had been lured out into the depths by the siren song of Olivia.

'Shivers,' he said. 'Oh shivers...speed skaters.' 'Black Night' continued to bang out. Doogles' podgy hand gripped my shoulders. His face screwed up in terror. 'Fuck a Duck. Speed skaters!'

I was scared; he was making me terrified. The speed skaters would smell our fear. I didn't know Douglas that well; only that his nickname was Doogles. And that he ate a lot. He was eating now. A thick devon sandwich. It was like some awful scene out of *Wild Kingdom*: a skinny deer and a fat deer had wandered too far out from the covering thickets; out where the predators waited. Out in the open. Speed skaters.

I panicked. 'Let go, Doogles!' I cried and tried to shake off his grip. He was clenching my T-shirt and holding onto his devon sandwich with the same hand. It was wrapped in rainbow-coloured grease-proof paper. Rainbow grease-proof paper – we were marked men. The more I struggled the tighter he gripped and the more he squashed his thick sandwich. I tried to push him off but he just leant into me. We started going faster. Speed skaters sneered past. One in a maroon and yellow shirt with a high collar called us wankers. He had very bad skin and was a very slow teller at the CBC bank in Margate. My nanna called him 'Pimply the Simpleton'. His name tag called him Gavin.

Doogles pushed forward and started running on his skates. My legs began to tremble. The sandwich began to turn into paste. I thought for an awful moment that I would be smothered by Doogles' body and be suffocated by his rainbow-clad devon goo.

I began to work my legs into frantic action. Doogles was so heavy and pushing so hard I could barely raise my skinny pins off the floor. I skated. We *both* did.

In fact we shot around the rink. Doogles' frantic whisper never far from my ear, the smell of sweat and devon never far from my nose. 'Fuck a duck, fuck a duck, fuck a duck.'

We went faster. We overtook Pimply the Simpleton and another angry-browed youth with a tattoo of an axe dripping blood on his arm. Deep Purple blazed. I farted. We sped. The odd person cheered. As we whizzed by I heard a girl scream, 'Go Fatty and Skinny!'

Of course it had to end. Hearing the cheers probably did it. A friend of mine called Kerry Videroni told me later that Doogles stuffed it up when he tried to wave at a girl. All he succeeded in doing, according to Kerry, was to over-balance and drop his devon bomb.

'We thought that he was gonna go arse over and pull you with him, but he grabbed your neck with his hand and you sorta managed to lean forward and pull him up.' Doogles had dropped his sandwich right in the path of Pimply the Simpleton and Blood Axe. To call what they suffered 'a stack' would be to understate on a grand scale. Put mildly, they were dinosaurs and Doogles' devon sandwich was the meteor.

They went arse up, then came down hard and fast and went spinning into the long, hard wooden bench that ran the length of one side of the rink. Fatty and Skinny rolled to a quiet stop not far from them.

Pimply looked like he was going to be sick. Blood Axe sat up slowly and shook his head. He smiled. I trembled and Doogles wheezed. Blood Axe had about three teeth in his head. He nodded and said, 'Youse fellas know ya tricks. Good stack, eh?'

I muttered something and left as quickly as I could. As I scurried outside I peered back through the wire to see what had become of Doogles.

He was talking to a long-jawed girl in a lime-green boob tube. Nonchalantly. Like some racing driver in a bad French film. Talking through his flying lap. Though instead of casually drawing back on a Gaulois he was polishing off what was left of his devon sandwich. Flicking away bits of hangover paste from his fingers. Nodding and pushing his glasses back on his face.

I have no idea what became of Doogles but that day, as I watched him through the rink's wire, he looked happy. That is how I remember him.

10

Not far from the old Rollerdrome was the Redcliffe jetty, an aging structure that reeked of the past. Literally and metaphorically. It held an odd grip on the people of the area because it was a reminder of the glory days – of steamers that would set out from Brisbane across the Bay filled with daytrippers and holidaymakers; of bored and moneyed American GIs during World War II who would tire of the town's amusements and would place wagers on how many planks a penny would roll along until it fell into the sea; of old songs sung in moonlight by couples who would walk out along the thin finger of wood there above the gentle waves.

The jetty was well into genteel decay when I came on the scene. But it was still the place to be. Halfway along this splinter of timber was an amusement parlour. It was rather oddly referred to as the halfway house. It had a dark, damp and creaky collection of slot machines on one side of the walkway and on the other a couple of pool tables. It was called Playland.

Because it was nearing the end of its existence, the little halfway house had a certain seedy richness that was haunting. The planks of the jetty were old and splintered and as the years had gone by the gaps between them had grown. You could look down between your toes and see the waves and the rippled sand of the seabed. I could almost feel the memory of the coin I held in my tight balled fist as it dug into my palm. Every child walked around with tight little fists. Not because they were looking for a fight but because they were holding on to their ten cent piece for dear life. If you dropped the coin it would certainly sleep with the fishes. Once I dropped a twenty cent piece. I looked down and then saw it bounce on the plank. Heard it bounce on the plank. And then saw it disappear through the darkness between gaps in the planking and appear on the other side, flipping down into the waves. The sun's rays caught it as it fell. The coin was a shiny sliver of silver spinning into the blue water below. I saw it hit the water and fall. I was almost convinced that I could hear it plop as it settled on the bottom of the sea. I stared after it without blinking.

I had just witnessed something quite beautiful and heartbreaking. I told my mother what had happened. I told her how lovely the coin had looked. 'Oh, well,' she said. 'You got your money's worth.' I told her I couldn't help feeling cheated. My father muttered from around the corner, 'Welcome to life, son.'

Out there in Playland nothing was certain and the sense of time being but a fleeting moment hung heavily in the air. This was illustrated in a rather disconcerting manner by the gentleman who was in charge of the place. It's not unreasonable to imagine that the man who ran an amusement parlour would be a jovial person, happy in the glee he helped give his customers. Perhaps he would even be wise in that beachcomber way, dispensing jewels of homely wisdom that he'd gleaned from the passing of the tides.

But Playland's ruler was a thin, grey streak of human misery. He'd stare at you through thick glasses with two-tone black and translucent frames. He'd flip through his paper, sometimes it was *The Courier-Mail*, but more often it would be the *Sporting Globe*, his long, thin and yellow-stained fingers holding a stubby pencil as he underlined his best bets. He'd roll his own with Ruby Capstan tobacco and glower at you as you went to the counter and asked for change. He'd growl if you complained how one of his machines had swallowed money and given nothing in return. Perhaps it was because we were children or perhaps he would do it to anybody, but we'd be dismissed with a wave of his arm. He'd gurgle from somewhere near the bottom of his long thin throat, 'No refunds.'

Perhaps not many children went out there by themselves. Certainly the poolroom was often filled with cigarette-smoking toughs, and the ruler of Playland would slide a sideways glance at the hoots and the language. But he'd never say anything or go to see what was going on. He was an old man dressed in a yellow-green cardigan and grey work shirt and trousers, parked out in a leaky shed above the sea. Marooned there in his halfway house with his old slot machines. Sometimes you'd hear him laugh and it sounded like he was clearing his throat, scarring its sides with a gurgling slag. He'd be laughing at some of his customers at the two-cent 'Test Your Strength' machine. It looked like something from Dr Frankenstein's lab. One hand would pull a handle while the other would rotate a crank that was connected to some kind of dynamo. The faster you'd rotate, the greater the electric shock you'd receive. This was Playland at its finest. Two-cent electric-shock therapy. Some of the toughs from the poolroom would wander over and have a go, jerking and shaking and swearing in their cracking adolescent voices. The cardiganed ruler would gurgle away with his best bets and his Ruby Capstans.

Outside Playland was an area from where you could dive or jump into the sea. An iron ladder led down into the waves and you could haul yourself up the rusty brown rungs and then climb on the wooden beams and throw yourself into the water. I was coordinated enough to dive but I would love to bomb. I'd tuck my skinny knees into a ball and leap into space and feel that emptying feeling in my stomach and balls as I hung in the air for a moment before falling.

If you ever saw people with cut-off jeans jumping or lolling around the ladder you'd know to keep a wide berth for they were the tough boys. Everyone would call them that. Big old chook-like ladies who'd be waiting for the red bus to Clontarf. They'd gather at the bus stop by the smelly toilets at the beginning of the jetty and cluck together as they sat in their billowing dresses, 'Toughs are out today. Those tough boys are lairing at Playland.'

One sunny afternoon the old chooks needn't have clucked: it was just some skinny kid and his podgy mate. Me and Reggie Worth were noisily bombing off the jetty. The water was pretty soupy and it was one of those days when the tides would sweep in and bring with them a flotilla of wobbling blue jellyfish. For some reason Reggie and I thought it would be fun to see how many we could bomb on.

I jumped into the gravy water and flapped to the surface. I saw him peering over Reggie's shoulder, a thin spiral of smoke streaming from his nose. The ruler of Playland. I slid jerkily up the ladder. His eyes never left mine. He inhaled on his fag and then spoke to me. As he spoke smoke streamed out.

'Are you old enough to be out here? You old enough to be bombing off the jetty... Your mother know you're here?'

I had never said boo to a grown-up. I would have been all of nine. But I'd been bombing jellyfish off the jetty and I felt pretty good. I looked at him. 'Get nicked, you old goose,' I heard myself say.

The ruler of Playland stared at me for a moment, then sighed a deep sigh and turned away, sucking on his cigarette. He looked very old. I said sorry, but if he heard he didn't answer. He just cleared his throat with a racking slag and a bit of a cough. He disappeared into the dark of Playland.

Not long after they closed it down. The wind and the sea were blowing it to bits. A storm finished it off. I never saw the ruler of Playland again. The Rollerdrome was razed to make a bigger Anzac Park and the council built a new, smaller jetty. People still stroll along it hand-in-hand at night, and kids still play and sing where the old Rollerdrome rink once sat.

Coastal development was a more recent phenomenon in Redcliffe. The housing estates had started inland and spread towards the shoreline. A victim of this steady march of housing was the drive-in, an entertainment facility that was so popular that it advertised in *The Courier-Mail*. 'People come from all over to go to the drive-in,' Mum would say proudly. For a while I believed that the Redcliffe Drive-in ranked alongside the Sydney Opera House and Ayers Rock as a major tourist attraction. One of the best things about the drive-in was that you didn't need to get dressed up to go. Unlike the flicks – even going down to the old Bay Cinema at Scarborough necessitated some form of sartorial effort. It was one of those airy old fibro palaces that reeked of another age. Most of us had to sit in vicious hard-backed leather chairs that smashed against each other when anyone who was sitting on one decided to go to the lolly bar or toilets, but at the back were the lovers' hammocks – rows of canvas double seats. People would grope and snog away to their heart's content because the bloke who ran the place never seemed that interested in shining his torch anywhere near them. He was a friend of my father's so we would occasionally get free tickets. This would mean we'd troop off as a family – and the way we behaved in the cinema was almost completely the same as we behaved at home.

My father revelled in it, and never once thought that yelling out and talking to the shadows on the screen was in any way outside the normal bounds of behaviour.

Once we went to see a re-issue of a James Bond film called *Doctor No* and Dad behaved as if it were a football match. He heaved and whistled and hooted and of course yelled out to James to 'Get the bugger now, Jimmy, kick him in the bread basket, man! God, Merv Cook could have done better!'

The fact that the double bills at the Bay were eccentric added to the enjoyment of going to the flicks with the family. One night we were hauled away to watch *Cleopatra Jones*, a blaxploitation kung-fu movie, and *All the Presidents Men*, an ultra-serious drama about the downfall of President Richard Nixon. We sat watching Cleopatra Jones fight her way through a burning casino. Dad had been fairly muted during the movie, content with sucking on a Morella Jube, but this came to a quick halt during a particularly clumsy fight scene. Suddenly, and for no apparent reason, a stupendously large pair of breasts appeared in front of the camera and jiggled about.

There was no head attached, just big jiggling breasts.

It was confronting, but Dad rose splendidly to the occasion.

'Christ! Look at them big TITS!' he roared. It reverberated around the cinema.

My mother sunk into the chair as best she could. 'Oh, Colin,' was all she said.

Unfortunately for my father, in his astonishment at seeing a three-storey sized pair of breasts he'd accidentally swallowed his Morella Jube and he began thumping himself with his great hammer-sized fists. He waved his hands. He grabbed his throat. He hauled at the row of seats in front of him. The whole cinema shook.

'Jube, jubes...jubes, jubes!' he gasped, and just when we thought it may have been serious, a jellied bullet rocketed from his mouth and flew into the hair of an old woman two aisles down.

We sat there in tears.

'Oh, Colin,' said my mother again.

'Bloody jube,' said my father.

A few years later I was up the back in the canvas hammocks with a girl and we passed Morella Jubes to and fro with only our mouths. The double bill was *Enter the Dragon* and *Grizzly*. The latter was about a radioactive grizzly bear who terrorised weekend campers. During a rather tense moment my date bit my tongue so hard that I thought she had chopped it in two.

'Sorry, sorry. I thought it was a jube,' she said.

Just then an actor on screen shouted out, 'Never trust a grizzly that's tasted human flesh!'

The drive-in was an epic kind of communal theatre. Mum and Dad would take their flat-top truck and we'd set up a trestle table and sit around in our pyjamas eating fish-finger sandwiches and drinking Milo while watching films like *The Love Bug*.

Dad had the handy habit of regularly driving off with the speaker still attached to the car door. The family record was six in one night. We went to watch a Charles Bronson movie called

The Mechanic about hitmen. The other movie was *Rollerball*, a futuristic sport adventure. We'd drive from spot to spot in our old Holden, shifting position like some great grazing beast intent on seeking the green grass of the drive-in.

'Right, this is simply not up to it,' said Dad and we'd be off, complete with the speaker attached to the car window. 'Christ, they really should design these things a bit better,' he mumbled. 'I think we got away with that,' he added. After a while my sister took over and she collected two, with my brother driving off with a solitary speaker to add to the tally.

A few years later, when the end was approaching for the drive-in, they did away with the speakers in an attempt to modernise the equipment, meaning you could tune in to the soundtrack of the movie with the FM radio in your car. This led to the 'Night of the Golden Torana'. The Golden Torana was in fact very gold, it was burnished gold; it shimmered and glowed. If Jason had been sent out to get a Golden Torana instead of the Golden Fleece this was the vehicle he and his Argonauts would have come looking for. It belonged to a friend of mine, Ricky Kheil. Ricky was a popular young man, in fact he was a bit of a celebrity because he was the first boy in high school to get his licence and to have a car. This was probably because he was older than us. He was a good bloke and could play rugby and was always up for a challenge. As far as being an intelligent and studious young man who dedicated himself to the betterment of his mind – Ricky was a good bloke and could play rugby.

Once he was challenged to eat a cake of soap and of course he did but he got about halfway through and bubbles started coming out of his nose. He ended up spending a couple of days in hospital. Another time he tried to pierce his own ear with a darning needle, a cufflink and a cigarette lighter – for sterilisation purposes only – in a maths class. All in all Ricky was a real renaissance man for he had a gift with languages. His speciality was 'Arpy Darpy'. I have never before or since met anyone who was as gifted in this ancient language, in fact I don't think I've ever met anyone who spoke this language. No, I don't think I have.

The basics of Arpy Darpy were to substitute a vowel with Arp or Darp – I wasn't quite sure which, but it didn't seem to make much difference, it all sounded the same to me. Ricky's finest Arpy Darpy moment came one wild Sunday afternoon on Moreton Bay. Returning from a week camping in the old pill boxes on Moreton Island, the low-slung cruise boat we were travelling on was caught in a violent swell that made the old boat tip at alarming angles.

'What a way to spend my birthday,' moaned an old lady as she clutched at the rail and hurled bits of her stomach into a rubbish bag provided to her by a panicked first mate.

'Ricky,' I said. 'Ricky, that woman's having her birthday.'

Ricky, who wore a sombrero, was standing staring out at the huge rolling waves. He turned and smiled.

'Your birthday today?' he asked the old dear pleasantly.

The woman hurled into the bag. Ricky moved over to her and shouted in her ear.

'Your birthday today?'

The poor woman turned to see this huge young man looming over her. She nodded.

'Bit crook?' asked Ricky, sounding like he was passing a major diagnosis.

The woman groaned and her husband, who was wall-eyed, shouted back. 'Well, what do you think?'

Ricky shrugged his shoulders and took a closer look. 'Oh yeah, that's no good,' he said and then smiled and pushed his giant sombrero back up his head and stood like an ocker Cisco the Kid. 'What you need is a song, for your birthday. Come on everybody, let's Arpy Darpy!' It was like a line from a bad Cliff Richard musical from the sixties, only it was a tad more surreal.

So there we were – the wall-eyed man with a comb-over hair cut; his vomiting wife with her head wrapped in a green rubbish bag like the Elephant Man, and Ricky, immense in a T-shirt and with his thighs exploding from his footy shorts, his sunburnt face as big as a melon topped off with an absurd multi-coloured straw sombrero. He swang his arms like a pirate singing a sea shanty and roared his song.

'Harpyppy Barpythdarpyy tarpy yarpyarpy…'

And so on.

It was almost as good a sight as his Golden Torana as we zoomed into the drive-in one night. Ricky asked for six tickets in Arpy Darpy as a joke and was told by the manager to 'get rooted, you silly monger'. It was a promising start to the evening.

The film playing was *Alien* and as we sat in the Golden Torana and twiddled with the FM radio to tune in the drive-in's band, Ricky stopped at the cricket.

'It's the cricket!' cried Ricky. 'It's the cricket!'

'Tune in the radio, Ricky,' I said.

'Don't you wanna listen to the cricket?' Ricky sounded bewildered.

'Listen, Ricky,' piped up Beetle O'Brien. 'We want to watch the film.'

'Suit yourselves,' said Ricky. He was silent for a few moments, his big hand resting on the dial. 'It's Australia versus the Windies!' Ricky shook his head.

'Come on, Ricky,' said Beetle.

'Farpyck Yarpyarpy,' muttered Ricky as he gave in. He never let go of his love for the cricket, and we all sat cringing in the car watching the Alien do its business to all the actors in the spaceship. We watched until Ricky could stand it no more. As Sigourney Weaver raced down a gantry way with her rifle and kitten, and the Alien slithered after her, fangs bared and talons swinging, shrieks exploded from cars all around the drive-in.

Ricky lurched forward, his hand twiddling the radio dial. 'It's my car, *my* car... The cricket, want to hear the cricket!' he declared.

Our protests fell on deaf ears and so we sat in the Golden Torana listening to Australia play the Windies while the Alien went after Sigourney. Strangely enough the sound seemed to suit the action on screen, and as some poor unfortunate astronaut was eaten by the monster, Ricky murmured, 'Bring back Lillee, come on, it's the only hope we've got.' The crowd at the Sydney Cricket Ground roared approval and for a few glorious moments the commentator's words worked in unison with the giant screen.

'Perhaps now's the time to bring back Lillee into the attack!' said Sigourney as she clenched a blaster and sounded uncannily like Jim Maxwell.

'Shit! She's right, even *she* says Lillee should bowl!' yelled Ricky.

As Sigourney finally killed the Alien, and Dennis Lillee was brought into the attack and bowled Michael Holding, Ricky cried, 'We've won by six runs!' and tooted his horn. 'That,' he cried, pointing to the screen, 'was a bloody good film. Why don't they make more like that?' He tooted his horn again and the crowd on the radio kept cheering and applauding. And as I sat in that restaurant years later I applauded too as the man in the white dinner jacket thanked the real estate man made-good for his speech.

At the next table was a man I vaguely knew from the council. 'Did you used to go to the drive-in?' I asked him.

He nodded. 'A few times, yeah.'

'Did you ever see *Alien* there at all?'

'Uh no, not that I can remember.'

'Oh, I did.'

He had a sip of his drink, tapped my arm and leant in. 'I actually used to live at the back of the drive-in when I was a kid,' he said.

'Really? Free movies in your front yard.'

He nodded. 'Yeah, but it got a bit toey towards the end when the bloke who ran it would stick the pornos on.'

'That would have been a bit rough.'

'Yeah, well they weren't hardcore or anything, but you know it was a bit stiff for the old folks to see bibs and bobs bouncing around up there. It was the only way he could make money in the end, I think. The poor bloke would put on about four in a row. Mum and Dad would take the dogs for a walk and they'd bump into all these pervs hiding behind the fence of the drive-in copping a free look!' He laughed a little and then continued. 'But it was silly to stick the porn on because you know, you can get all the hardcore stuff posted to you and just play it on your telly. No need for an outdoor session.' He laughed again. 'Although people did spend a lot of time on their verandahs.'

I nodded. Then I applauded.

11

Applause continued as the man in the white dinner jacket mentioned a few people who owned shops along the waterfront, who had donated some of the gifts that were being given away that night.

The beach and the shopping strip was changing. Pubs were being ripped down and modernised. Pastel palaces with poker machines. Appropriate Development.

In an attempt to maintain a 'more authentic historical feel' Redcliffe's local historical society had taken to running heritage tours, visiting sites of historical significance. The only problem was that most of the sites no longer existed; somehow they had metamorphed into more Appropriate Development. But they had plaques. People would get out of a small bus and parade around on the tour viewing plaques on Crisis Shoe Liquidators or a bus stop or Quality Budget Autos. The bus would drive around the streets with the tour guide and a hairy mumbling driver looking for something vaguely historical. The guide was a tidy little woman with tortured dyed hair who spoke into a microphone. Occasionally. She knew about as much history of the Peninsula as Genghis Khan knew about canasta. Her running commentary centred on how much this or that house went for, what development was going up here and how well disciplined the children from a fundamentalist Christian school were.

At least until the bus stopped outside a wooden house in Scarborough. It didn't take long to work out why.

There, hanging from a cotton tree in the front yard was a sign, letters burnt into treated pine: 'Bee Gees'. This was where the Gibb boys had lived. The sign had a familiar look; the slightly emaciated and spindly 'S' made me immediately think of the Cascades.

Other recent attempts to celebrate the town's past included an initiative from the Chamber of Commerce and the council to bring back to life a beauty contest, a homage to the 1950s competitions that were held at Suttons Beach. Various workers from local businesses poured themselves into gowns and swimmers in the revived Sungirl Quest. Some sad-faced old pop star from the seventies came and sang, and the Sungirls waddled around in 'swim suits' to songs that were just as trite and meaningless as they were the first time they were screeched by our former Queen of Pop on *Countdown*. Nobody seemed to think it was a bad idea.

•

They also thought it was a good idea when the civic spirit continued with a First Settlement festival parade. I stood with my children and watched it. Leading the pack was the local dramatic society, made up almost entirely of English immigrants in costume; then a bellowing Town Crier rang his bell and sounded like a demented creature from *Star Wars*. Very well-fed convicts and baggy-trousered guards brought up the rear. The guards beat the porky convicts with whips and plastic gun butts. It was strange; people out for a morning stroll watching mock brutalisation.

'Should we be clapping this, Dad? Is he hurt?' my son asked.

'Uh, I think that's the idea, mate,' I said, looking around to make sure. Everyone was applauding enthusiastically so we joined in, celebrating our local history.

Then came a 'history of transport', or, as the poster said, 'a cavalcade of the history of transport': a man dressed as a soldier on a horse; an old truck; a taxi that had just driven from the nearby rank; and a Bongo van. This is where things went a little odd. The Bongo van was advertising one of the local papers and on the roof was a figure reclining on a chair reading the local newspaper. Well, that was fine. But the figure just happened to be a blow-up sex doll. Why not? Couldn't put a real person up there, so get a blow-up doll. Just stop by the adult shop, Naughty but Nice, next door to the newspaper office, blow up one of the dolls, gaffer tape her by her elbows and ankles to a piece of outdoor furniture and plonk her on the roof of the Bongo van. She was wearing a nylon, flowery dress that older women who sell homemade jams and condiments and craft on charity stalls might wear. The newspaper was taped to her wrists while her mouth was an open O. There was a bit of a breeze about and the tape had come loose on one ankle and so instead of enjoying the paper, she seemed to be squirming rather immodestly. As the floral dress flapped up and down and the leg pointed to all angles of the compass, the crowd just stared.

'That looks like an Osti dress; I like Osti dresses,' said an old lady in front of us.

A man in the Bongo van leant out the window, held up an air horn and blew a long hooting howl. Just at that moment a gust blew the dolly's dress up.

'Yes, definitely an Osti,' nodded the old woman.

Next was a four-wheel-drive Monster truck called the Devastator, with huge, massively over-inflated and out-of-proportion wheels. Apparently it was a part of a dynamic show playing the next night at the Redcliffe Trotting Track. Speakers blared that the Devastator could 'wreck a family sedan in thirty seconds. Yeah, squash it like a bug!'

The Devastator was followed by a collection of bearded, middle-aged men on thundering Harley Davidsons. They had their middle-aged biker girlfriends squashed onto the seats behind them, and they looked like those bikers from the Clint Eastwood movie *Any Which Way But Loose*. Clint was a bit old and needed people to beat up who were older and greyer and fatter than he was, so we especially enjoyed the *Any Which Way But Loose* biker gang.

In a fitting finale to this extravaganza, two purring invalid scooters brought up the rear, their drivers coughing and wheezing through the exhaust of the *Any Which Way But Loose*'ers and the Devastator.

What a parade. I looked out to the sea, scratched my head and took the kids to have an ice-cream in one of the arcades.

As middle teenagers with not much else to do, my friend Peter Bolton and I would love to walk along the strip and down the long dark arcades. We'd drop by a second-hand book and comic exchange and see what we could pick up. I'd trawl in search of supremely awful war comics that I could laugh at. To do this I needed capital but thanks to my father and his love of auctions, I had an almost unlimited source of gold. My old man had picked up a case of books that had been marked as faulty and had dumped them in the shed and left them there. 'Got 'em for five bucks. Don't know what they are.'

The case contained a seemingly endless number of an 'international bestseller', according to its cover. It featured a balding man with a big moustache and a very big smile. Its title explained its eager acceptance at the book exchange: *Your Erogenous Zones*. Old baldy on the cover was some American psychologist who I guess would help explain where your erogenous zones were located and then what to do with them. The lady with the dyed hair and chook-bum mouth at the book exchange would hold these books as if they were some rare prize, and sure enough when I returned she would have placed Old Baldy's book in the Adult section.

She could hardly contain herself. 'More copies of that... that... book?' she said.

'Yes... three.' I slowly revealed them to her.

Her hands trembled. 'They sell well,' she whispered. She could be scary sometimes, like Gollum from *The Lord of the Rings*. 'Oh, my precious,' she'd say.

It was like I was a dealer in dirt. Should I have felt somehow soiled that dirty books where being peddled openly by myself? I couldn't believe my luck.

'Why in God's name would anybody buy this shit?' Peter Bolton asked me one day as I took a few more copies down to the exchange.

'No idea, but it's gold!'

I was curious, though, and so sought information.

'Hey, who buys this book?' I asked Mrs Gollum.

'Oh, this book?' she said and smiled slyly. 'This book is very popular. Lots of people buy this book.' And then she laughed to herself. 'All sorts of people.'

'Okay.' I nodded and walked over to search for bad war comics.

Although the copies were marked as 'faulty', as far as I know nobody ever complained. They sold well and I liked to think that people all over the Peninsula were achieving orgasmic satisfaction when they scratched their elbow or patted the back of their skull. I looked around the restaurant now and thought, as I had another drink, that there's a good chance some of these people here, on this night of nights, may have actually bought one of those faulty copies of *Your Erogenous Zones*. I looked at the mayor and the bloke in the white dinner jacket and the sharp-faced owner–manager. *I know your secrets.*

But one day the books ran out and Mrs Gollum had to do without her Precious.

We would still wander through the arcades, though. They were long and dark and bursting with an interesting collection of human flotsam. Redcliffe was a small town but the arcades seemed to us to be filled with the look-a-likes of famous faces.

'Maybe this is where they come to die,' I said to Peter. 'Maybe they're the real McCoy.'

'No, I don't think so. Some of these people have been dead for a long time.'

We laughed. 'Okay, so this is where they come when they're dead.'

There was an old man who was the spitting image of Spencer Tracy in *The Old Man and the Sea*. He'd wander the streets chewing and carrying a phalanx of plastic bags. Arthur 'Cocky' Calwell was of a similar vein and was the doppelgänger of the former Labor leader. He would shuffle up and down Comino's Arcade talking to the reflections of himself. Malcolm Fraser sold second-hand furniture in a lane off Sutton Street. Fernando Lamas, aka *The Love Boat*, was an old chap in his sixties who'd saunter about the shops in sunglasses and high-hitch black Speedos. David Niven was a woman with a moustache who worked in the newsagency. Tarzan was a tanned man with long blond hair and a wild-man outlook on life. He'd parade up and down the strip bare chested and yelling, while his father, who was the parking inspector, would look away.

Suddenly I was dragged back to reality and was on my feet, shaking hands with the real estate man made-good. It was the mayor's turn and he said how proud he was of this town, of this night, and of the history of this wonderful city by the sea. There was more applause and it sounded like rain again. I forgot about the girl I kissed on the beach and remembered another rainy night. Just behind the mayor's head, through the window, I could see the Kentucky Fried Chicken restaurant in the distance. I'm fairly sure it was one of the first in Australia and when it opened they installed a merry-go-round in the car park. I'd go there regularly with Reg Worth and we'd never tire of hearing the epic order 'two buckets of chicken'. And we would stop halfway up the hill, by the house with the lantana, and share a piece each from the buckets. But on one occasion, Reg rasped that tonight he wanted, 'A barrel of chicken... With extra gravy!' No pretence of anything fancy; just food, fried and flung into a bucket.

Atop the restaurant was a Colonel Sanders weather vane. The Southern American Colonel in a white suit and shirt and black shoe-string tie, his walking cane held at a jaunty angle pointed to the wind, became a bit of a talking point in Redcliffe.

Remember, it was a small town.

Late one night, a long time past the bucket-snitching years, a group of us sat around a Laminex kitchen table, drinking and singing. We had just attempted 'American Pie'; then someone wanted to sing 'Hotel California'. Half of us tried. Suddenly I thought of the Colonel. Years of climatic abuse had rusted him solid. Instead of following the breezes he was jauntily frozen, his cane pointing towards the Southern Cross on a clear night. Pointed with a smug assuredness of ownership. Listening to one of the more ludicrous popular songs sung by out-of-it drunks spurred me to a great decision.

Fuck all this American shit. Fuck the Eagles. And fuck the Colonel. I'm getting him. And so that is how I found myself in the middle of a thunderstorm, drunk and dressed in a long blue fireman's coat and wearing (for concealment) a full-face balaclava, on top of the Kentucky Fried Chicken outlet singing a mixture of 'American Pie' and 'Hotel California' to a rusty Colonel Sanders. I'd borrowed the balaclava from an elder brother of a friend. He was known as Olsbro. As in Olive's brother. Olsbro had sewn plastic sunglass shades into the balaclava and as a consequence I could only see a little less than nothing.

I wrenched the Colonel. He wouldn't budge. I flicked back my sunglassed beanie and heaved with all my strength, grunting the Eagles dirge. And he came with me. Lifted free. And as I held him aloft, above me the sky opened. There, in the heavens, blazed the Southern Cross. I shrieked. My little band of followers below, some stationed around a green Gemini, paused and then returned my howls.

'We have the Colonel! Welcome to our Hotel California!' I held him aloft like a trophy. The sky closed and a huge crack of thunder rent the air. I overbalanced and just as I fell

I can remember seeing the lights of trawlers blinking at me. The Colonel and I slid down the wide corrugated roof and then rolled clanking onto the flat awning. Miraculously I was unhurt. 'We still have him!' I cried.

My band were happy. Over the next few weeks we held the Colonel captive down in the shed. We popped him on top of the Anzac memorial but nobody noticed. We thought about putting him on top of a church, but nobody could be bothered. I wrote a letter to the local paper saying the Colonel was being held by the Woody Point Canasta Club. The paper didn't publish or respond to the letter. After a while Peter Bolton and I made super-8 films starring the Colonel. *Psycho Sanders*. The good Colonel being loaded up a cattle ramp and hanged from a tree on my sister's deer farm. Then we got bored. I don't know what happened to him. The Colonel wasn't missed. He may not have pointed to the Southern Cross any more but people didn't care. They still bought their buckets of chicken.

The mayor spoke haltingly but smiled a lot. He wore a fancy Dan waistcoat. He looked around the room and pointed people out; waved to them, a bit like Forrest Gump. He welcomed somebody from the RSL and marvelled at how the club had grown to become a world-class entertainment facility. The man from the RSL had the grace to look a little embarrassed. The RSL certainly had a vast array of jingling pokies on parade just to the left of the Coral Sea Lounge. This was where you could fetch yourself a roast dinner on

Wednesday or Thursday nights. On Fridays, squashed against the thick high windows that looked out over the Coles car park, some poor duo would play pop songs.

I once saw some world-class entertainment in the Kokoda Track Room: an Elvis impersonator who had arrived from Las Vegas bearing the title of 'the world's best Elvis'. The honour had been bestowed upon him by Elvis Presley's former cook and I guess she would know an Elvis worth voting for when she saw one. He swivelled and hooted about and sang 'Hound Dog' underneath a Lest We Forget banner. He had a hairy nose and lovely voice.

In my youth, Anzac Day wasn't such a big deal. It was viewed at best as a day off; if it coincided with a weekend then that was a bonus. It was a day when my father and his kind would press their suits and shine their shoes the night before then mysteriously disappear. One year I heard Dad leaving; the house was dark and quiet, and the only noise was Dad whistling an old tune as his steps crackled down the drive. The tune was 'Always'.

Occasionally Mum would take us to see the march, and we'd watch Dad walk gravely past holding the black ribbon of remembrance, his medals dancing on his chest.

When I was older my friends Peter Bolton and Beetle O'Brien would buy a few tall bottles of beer from the bottle-o man, who wore thick glasses and had warts all over his arms, at the Ambassador Hotel. We'd then head into Redcliffe for the day's activities. These were glorious social occasions, out back of the RSL. Old Diggers and an assembled collection of prominent citizenry would howl in delight over a game of two-up and ambitious local aldermen and state parliamentarians would prowl around making sure they were seen.

Later, when Peter and I went upstairs, a group of similarly aged youths were asked to leave the RSL Club because of their uproarious behaviour. They'd been pushing and shoving amongst themselves. An old Digger who'd been marshalling the day's events in his uniform and slouch hat stepped over to the boys and barked, 'You lads can't fight in here, not now, not on Anzac Day.'

We thought this was most amusing and laughed so loudly that we too were shown the door. As we left, an old man who had been wandering about muttering to himself looked at us with tears in his eyes and said, 'Are you happy now, you bastards? Are you happy now?'

I think of Dad holding his ribbon of remembrance, of how he wouldn't smile at us as we waved to him. Peter and I weren't laughing at the old man in the RSL or his memories, we were just being young, thinking that life goes on and on.

Today we know it doesn't. Life ends. Sometimes in places far away, in a market place, in a schoolyard, at a checkpoint, in a war zone.

I have another sip of my drink and decide to go to the toilet.

12

On my way to the toilet my arm is grabbed and I'm stopped by someone from the *Redcliffe Herald*.

'Hello,' he says.

'Hello.'

'Hello, I'm from the *Redcliffe Herald*.'

'Yes,' I say.

'Yes,' he says.

'I'm going to the toilet.'

'Okay,' he says and pats me on the back.

The information contained in the *Redcliffe Herald* regularly stretched the limits of Mum's maternal love for me. I was the youngest of her children and by her accounts took the longest time to get here. Whenever I'd do something stupid, which I must admit was quite often, she'd eyeball me and declare, 'Nineteen hours I took to have you, *nineteen* hours, and for what?' These words were never more venomously uttered than the time when I placed my own obituary in the local paper. For some reason they published it.

William Mathews mourns the loss of Darrell William McInnes
Killed accidentally by a Zurich Zoo Truck
While serving with the Swiss Navy.

I had no idea it had been published until I heard Mum booming out across the road at me. 'I'm not talking to you, Deadman! Don't think a corpse is sitting in my house eating my food... You stupid boy...nineteen hours for what? A corpse!' She waved a copy of the *Herald* at me as she stomped off down towards the paper's offices.

'Where are you going?' I shouted.

'Off to the paper to tell them you're alive and a bloody idiot!'

'I thought you weren't talking to me?'

'You should go and see a doctor!' she screamed.

She didn't cook me any dinner that night and she wouldn't talk to me. Dad had no idea what was going on.

'Where's Cabbagehead's dinner? He's not on some stupid diet is he?'

'Who are you talking about?' hissed my mother.

'Him,' said my father, pointing at me with his knife. 'Him, that piecan there.'

'I don't see anybody.'

Dad put down his knife and fork. 'All right, what did you do to your mother? Have you been wearing those stupid bloody hairnets again?'

'Oh, I could come at the hairnets. The hairnets were nothing compared to this.' She handed him a copy of the paper.

He slowly read out the entry to himself. He actually thought it was a great joke and in time Mum came around too, and I was allowed to re-enter the world of the living.

As I enter the toilets I can hear the mayor reverently talking about the canal developments at Scarborough. These developments somehow turned muddy foreshores into dead-end alley million dollar mansions on the water. Some were large mock Tudor houses, some were large mock Queenslander houses. Some were beautiful homes. But they were all big and swollen. Were they any worse or better than the splintery fibro shacks they'd replaced? I didn't know what to think. I turned to the urinal and snuggled into a gap between two stocky men in expensive suits with tight collars.

Disappearing into the cubicle was a businessman I recognised who advertised liberally on the local community radio station. He dealt mainly in property development. He also dealt in some of the most remarkable noises I have ever heard in a public toilet. I imagine he was unbuckling his belt at about the same time I was preparing myself. He sounded like the Lone Ranger unbuckling his spurs and gunbelt, then going on to give Silver, his stallion, a bit of a pat. 'Whhhooooa, boy.'

'Jesus Christ Almighty,' I muttered.

The stocky man on my right elbowed me in the ribs. It was a practised effort and it nearly knocked me into the trough. I looked at him.

He was smiling. 'Fuck me dead, Billy, how are you, you long string of pelican shit?'

I looked at him. It was an old rugby coach of mine.

'G'day, Ray.'

'How are ya?' he said.

'Pretty good,' I said.

'Ahhhhhhhhhh...' said the Lone Ranger.

'You've done all right for yourself,' said Ray. He offered me his hand to shake. I shook it. It flew in the face of practised personal hygiene but an old mate is an old mate.

'Yeah, can't complain,' I said.

Ray laughed and shook his head. We shook hands again, I nodded, and we peed. The Lone Ranger groaned as if he were lifting an enormous weight.

'Good night,' said Ray.

'Sure is.'

'Yeahhh,' growled the Lone Ranger.

Ray was the coach who, for me, summed up rugby so well in one blistering halftime address. 'Christ!' he screamed. 'You bastards are playing like a pack of poofters!' His eyes had narrowed. 'No, it's worse than that. You're playing like a pack of *women*!'

I looked at him and remembered that he had three daughters.

For the next game he tried a new method of motivation and he attempted to fuse a number of inspirational sources to lift us to victory. Anybody who has played team sport will know that sooner or later a coach will try to use material to gee up and inspire his or her players. Quoting history and reinterpreting it in terms of sport, especially Anzac Day, is often on the cards. Movies like the *Rocky* series are shown; music to pump up the adrenaline is played.

Ray always thought big, and he aimed for the stars with this particular effort, even though it might have been a bit rushed. It came to him while he was watching television: a film came on and he sensed that it had the tone to lift his team, so he must have hurriedly gone and fetched a tape recorder and placed it by the television to record the music. The film was *The Guns of Navarone*, a hoary old adventure that moves like the clappers and was a regular top-ten pizza night flick. It was a favourite in our house, even Dad liked it, which was odd because he usually didn't have much time for war movies.

'This one's all right,' he'd say. 'Even if they do run like pansies.'

'Gregory Peck is not a pansy,' Mum would offer indignantly.

'I didn't say Gregory bloody Peck was a pansy, I said he *ran* like a pansy. He's all floppy with his arms and he moves like he's got a broom up his arse.'

'Colin.'

'Well, he does.'

'Well, you're just jealous.'

'I'm not jealous of having a broom up my arse.'

'Colin! Now do you want a cup of tea with this film or not?'

'Yes, all right, it's a cracker.' Then he'd clap his hands and yell, 'Come on, Broom Bum, let's see what you've got!'

The film was about the World War II mission to destroy some big guns in a cliff that could destroy Allied ships. It was set in Greece and had a rousing music score. When you got past the way the actors ran, it was indeed a fine film.

Watching the actors haul themselves up some mountain I turned to Dad and tried to rag him. 'Is this what the war was like, Dad?'

He sipped on his tea. 'Yes, son, men in bad wigs and moustaches climbing papier-mâché rocks is a pretty fair description of warfare. You bloody drongo.'

Unknown to me, as I was watching the film with my family, Ray was busily recording the soundtrack. Next morning when I sat with my team mates on the hard wooden benches in the change rooms of the footy club, Ray plonked a heavy black tape recorder in the middle of the floor.

'Right boys,' he said. 'Listen to me...now shut your eyes...'

Dutifully we shut our eyes and the liniment and goanna oil that had been spread over our thighs and calves smelt even stronger. For a while there was silence. I expected to hear one of Ray's usual warm-up inspirational tunes like 'Black Betty' or 'High Voltage Rock and Roll'.

Then the tape recorder hissed into life.

An ad for Leo Muller Toyota, a car dealer in Brisbane, started playing. It consisted of a woman's high and willowy voice echoing the car yard's name.

Ray had picked up all the ads as well as almost every sound in his house. 'Don't listen to this bit,' he said as he dismissed

Leo Muller Toyota. 'This has got nothing to do with the game… This! Listen to this!'

The film had begun. Rousing orchestral music began playing, followed by a prologue spoken by a fruity old actor who rolled his R's alarmingly.

Grrrrrrrrrreece and the islands of the Aegean Sea have given birth to many myths and legends of war and adventure.

'Myths, legends, the ancient gods of Greece. It's our adventure today, boys, we'll make war today…' Ray intoned. These words were delivered in the gaps between the fruity actor's rumbling delivery. Ray had a flat nasal voice and the whole exchange was quite bizarre. It was like a couple talking over each other while telling the same story at a dinner party.

'And these once prrrrrrroud stones, these rrrruined and shattered temples.'

As the actor rolled on, another voice was heard. It was Ray's wife.

'Ray!' she shouted from another room.

'Yes,' Ray's voice whispered in answer.

'Ray! Are you there? RAY!' she yelled.

'Yes!' Ray screamed in a whisper.

'Bear witness to the once prrrroud civilisation that flourrrrished and then died here.'

'Died here, today, the once proud reputation of Norths–Teachers dies today here!' roared Ray in the clubhouse.

'Ray? What are you doing?' It was Ray's wife again. 'Are you watching TV?'

'Sshhh, I'm just taping something.'

'Ray, the girls have to go, are you ready?'

'Hang on, Donna.'

'*Two grrrrreat rrrrradar contrrrrolled guns rrrruled the strrrraights of Navarrrrone.*'

'Yes great guns, gun players that will fall today,' said Ray. His tone suggested he was having second thoughts about his motivation session.

'Ray, the girls have to go to the concert, hurry up. Please!'

'All right, all right.'

'And do your fly up properly, Ray. Please,' said Donna as politely as she could.

'*Without evacuation, the men on the island of Kyrrross would be doomed. Time was rrrrrunning out.*' Music jangled behind the narrator, adding urgency to his words.

'Hurry up, Daddy!' two little voices pleaded.

'All right, Cherie, come on, Melinda. Daddy's just doing something for the footy.'

'Footy!' whinged one of the girls.

The music swelled.

Donna shouted. 'Have you fed Banjo, Ray?'

'What?' Ray was beside himself.

'Just think of the game, fellas, time to think of the game,' Ray implored us in the clubhouse now.

'Have you fed Banjo?' said Donna as if talking to an idiot.

'Yes...yes. I've fed the dog!'

The music was building ever more threateningly.

'Then why is he doing that to the couch?' asked Donna sweetly.

'Banjo's doing naughties on the couch!' said one of the girls.

A slobbering noise grew louder.

'*What happened in the next six days…*' The narrator paused for dramatic effect.

There was a thump and then a yelp.

'Daddy hit Banjo!' both girls chimed in.

Banjo barked and whimpered. There were sounds of him being comforted.

'All right, let's go,' Ray said on the tape recorder. A door closed.

'*Became known as the legend of Navarrrrone!*' The music exploded.

Ray screamed at us. 'The legends! Here we go. Our day to make a name for ourselves… Let's go!'

As we shuffled out dumbfounded, Ray roared, 'The Guns of Navarone, boys! The Guns of Navarone.'

We got absolutely slaughtered.

'How are your daughters, Ray?' I asked in the loos.

Ray nodded. 'Good, they're good. All grown up now.'

'And Donna?'

'God, yeah, she's good,' he said with a smile.

'You still got the place in Scarborough?'

Ray nodded while the Lone Ranger practised scales on his French Horn. Ray zipped up his fly and washed his hands. 'Yeah…yeah. Big empty mausoleum. When the kids leave, mate, they make anything empty. Nice views, though.'

'What about Banjo?'

Ray stopped and looked at me. 'Banjo!' He shook his head and his big belly laughed. 'Banjo, bloody old Banjo. He was a shocker. No, he's buried out the back of the house...he was a funny bloody mutt.' He paused. 'You know the house isn't that empty. Filled with good memories. Just like tonight.'

I asked him if he still did legal aid work. He shook his head. 'No, Billy, no. That's a young fella's game.' He pointed towards the Lone Ranger's cubicle. 'I work for the fella who's giving birth to the baby elephant out the back of his arse. Good luck with the speech, mate.'

He clapped me on the shoulder and walked off the way old rugby players do. Before he disappeared, he turned and smiled. 'Guns of Navarone, Billy!' He winked and was gone.

I washed my hands and smiled as I looked in the mirror. I laughed. I saw something sticking out of my suit pocket; it was the business card from the driver of the funeral car. I looked at his smiling face. 'The night of nights,' he'd said. I put the card back in my pocket. 'The night of nights,' I said to myself.

The Lone Ranger let rip something akin to one of the Guns of Navarone going off. I opened the door and left him howling alone in the toilet.

'And they still love Redcliffe, the city by the sea!' It was the mayor again. 'All those people who used to come here on the paddle ships, perhaps their grandchildren and great grandchildren are coming back to the Peninsula. Our next speaker is someone who's come back again tonight, and not by paddle boat.'

211

I had another quick drink. I had never felt less like speaking. A hand slapped me on the back. It was the real estate man made-good. 'I love this place... Goodonyou, goodonyou.'

I stood up and walked to the podium past a table where a man who had just bought an island resort sat applauding and smiling at me. Earlier in the night I had heard someone say how they had enjoyed the outdoor cinema on this resort. 'Yeah, yeah, we'll make it better... Forty-foot pornos under the stars!' It was a joke.

A federal MP who sat applauding at the next table had laughed with him. 'Oh, there's an entrepreneur born every minute.' I'm pretty certain 'family values' were part of her election platform.

I stood at the podium and went through my notes. I looked at these people. They had grown up here just like me. They had seen the same things I'd seen. They were here in the swankiest restaurant in town because they saw change in the air. It was their town, their home, and they didn't need any help from anybody else to live their lives. This town where I grew up was changing. It was getting something it had never had: rich people. The people in this room were growing richer and richer; land by the coast was a saleable thing. Change. They were riding change for whatever it was worth.

Change is life. That is what my father said.

'You can't stop change, mate. You can't stop it. People have tried and all it did was bring a lot of misery. If it happens, it happens.'

I stood and looked at them all, and caught the eye of the woman who I'd ridden the bus with all those years ago. She didn't look fifteen anymore, but then again somehow she did. I wondered if she still wore the same perfume and if the applause reminded her of rain on a tin roof and a sweet but clumsy kiss on the beach to the strains of Bill and Boyd.

I thought of Spencer Tracy and 'Cocky' Calwell and Dad and Uncle Reg. I thought of the ruler of Playland and I thought of Josey Kanga and wondered how his English was and if he still liked Australian girls. I thought of that man in the German helmet and his Christmas shirt and wondered if he ever got to the banana trees.

The real estate man nodded. I suddenly understood that these people were just people who lived in a town I'd known. They were here to remember, to remember the land and the way it was. Then they were going to go on living their lives. I believed the real estate man when he said he loved this place. He was a good man. He had given a staggeringly generous donation to the museum.

The guest of honour thought of one other person as he began his speech. With a whisper to himself, 'Welcome to the Hotel California.' And then louder to the audience... 'It's a lovely place...such a lovely place.'

Saying
Goodbye

13

The moment I saw her, I knew it was time for saying goodbye.

The paramedics brought Aunty Rita from the ambulance in that unhurried, practised way that routine breeds. They chatted and exchanged hellos with another pair of ambos who leant against the doorway smoking. As they wheeled her through the entrance to the emergency ward, one of the men smoking said, 'Long day, today.'

The other nodded. 'Yeah. Long day.'

I walked over to her and called her name. 'Aunty Rita.'

One of the paramedics looked at me. Perhaps it sounded strange that a grown man would address someone as 'aunty', but she was always Aunty Rita to me. Or perhaps it was the tone of my voice.

The other man quietly told me to wait for the doctor in the foyer. I nodded and watched my aunt disappear down the hallway. I stood there for a little while, long enough to see the man stub out his cigarette.

'Better get back to it,' he said as he climbed up into the ambulance. He whistled a few bars of 'Don't Worry, Be Happy', coughed a couple of times, and then drove off. The exhaust lingered, mingling with the cigarette smoke, curling skywards in dark wisps.

Why I didn't go inside immediately I don't know. Perhaps I thought I'd get in the way.

Perhaps I heard the voices of my mother and her sister.

'Oh, get out of the way!' Aunty Rita would often say, laughing her big, rumbling laugh.

'What are you after now?'

'Don't hang on the fridge door.'

'Don't lean.'

'Oh, you are an awful boy...'

'For goodness sake, push off.'

I heard the intercom from the wards and as I walked down the hallway towards Emergency, I heard a magpie calling. I hoped somehow my aunt could hear it too. I knew it was time to say goodbye.

Earlier that day, a friend of Mum's had phoned with the news that Aunty Rita had suffered a stroke and was being taken to the Redcliffe Hospital. After she put down the phone my mother turned to me. 'Please can you go to the hospital? Please. I'll look after the kids. But can you just go?'

I nodded. I knew why she couldn't go, just yet.

The ambulance men didn't know how long Rita had been on her own. Mum had invited her to go to the movies with us; my children and I were visiting. But she never came.

Aunty Rita lived near Redcliffe on the mudflats of Deception Bay in a house that my father had built for her, on a small farm. Dad found the land for her, but my mother always liked to remind him that it had a lot to do with Dean Martin.

Visiting was usually a day trip and just getting there was often an adventure in itself. We never had a car that you could call 'family friendly'. Dad's trucks behaved themselves (in spite of his appalling driving), but as far as cars were concerned, there was never really one that fitted the picture of a shiny family sedan. This would often mean that if we were to travel off the Peninsula, to go into the outside world, the journey was inevitably fraught with danger.

'Jesus, I feel like Charles Kingsford bloody Smith in this heap!' my father said once as we drove across the bumpy bridge to watch a game of rugby in North Brisbane.

My mother liked Smithy. 'Well, he nearly always got where he was going, so what's wrong with that?' she said.

'Oh, Riss, please, Kingsford Smith ended arse up in the Bay of bleeding Bengal. And he always had some poor sod hanging on to his oil tin out on the bloody wing.'

'Charles Ulm,' said my mother.

'All right, Charles Ulm. But I'm just saying that if Charles Ulm was in this bucket of tripe there'd be a good chance of him being spreadeagled on the bonnet with his wherewithal.'

'Why?' said my sister.

'Oh, for crying out bleeding loud!' roared Dad above the racket of the engine. 'Do I have to paint it out to you?'

'It might help.'

'All I'm saying is that this...car, if you can call it that, is –'

Mum began to laugh.

'Riss, please.' But Dad had started too.

'What, you silly bloody man?' my mother said, laughing more.

'This car is fraught with danger and if you don't all behave I'll have you Charley Ulming out there on the bonnet!' My father turned to Mum. 'Let's try a bit of Morse.' He then proceeded to beep the horn in fits and starts as we lurched over the Hornibrook's lumps. 'We don't want to end up having to Fred Flintstone it there.'

That was my father's term for having to push a car when it had stopped. Like the caveman cartoon cars that were powered by Fred or Barney's flying feet.

My mother loved Volkswagen Beetles. Mainly because they were so small you could park them just about anywhere. 'They're such a dear little car,' she would coo as her great family of six-footers would crumple themselves into tiny balls to fit inside the small cramped bubble cars.

These cars added lustre to my mother's career as being a doppelgänger for Jon Pertwee's Doctor Who. Like the Time Lord with his shock of white hair, zooming around in his telephone-box spaceship the Tardis, Mum would hoon around in her beloved Beetle. When the car whined and moaned into life it sounded so much like the noise the Tardis made that the name soon stuck. In fact, like the Tardis of *Doctor Who* the Beetle Tardis of my mother's also had elastic dimensions inside. How else could people explain why so many big McInneses and their noisy dogs could fit into so small a space.

It was in the Beetles that we would go on some of our most popular holiday outings: shopping centre openings. Wherever there was an opening, we would be there. The Chermside K-Mart, the Strathpine Myer, the Indooroopilly Shopping Town and, of course, Toombul Shopping Town were all on the hit list for Mum's Tardis. Back in the seventies, there was nothing more exciting that heading off across the Hornibrook to the big 'T' of the Toombul Shopping Town.

My mother and Aunty Rita would be amazed at the amount of shops under one roof.

'Do you think it will last, Reet?' Mum asked Aunty Rita once.

'It's the way of the future, Iris. It's as modern as tomorrow.' Aunty Rita shook her head at us running around like caged lunatics in the big steel rocket that was stuck out in the back car park. 'As modern as tomorrow,' she said again, then sat bolt upright and pointed at a bulky man with a comb-over hairstyle dressed in a safari suit. He wasn't a member of the Labor Party but he dressed like one. 'It's Mick Cox, Mick Cox,' she boomed. He was off the telly and a favourite of hers because he hosted the greyhound segment on *Sportscene* on Channel Seven every Sunday. 'Here's the man with all the headlines and excitement from the wonderful world of greyhounds and the Gabba!' boomed his introduction. Mick

Cox stared at us and blinked a bit. What else do you do? Two grown women were waving and yelling at him and nearby there was a steel-cage rocket filled with children who were yelling, 'Here's the man with all the headlines and excitement from the wonderful world of greyhounds and the Gabba!'

'You see, even the stars come to Toombul to shop! It's as modern as tomorrow,' said Rita.

The Volkswagens were the most trustworthy vehicles in what was a very odd and distinctly untrustworthy family fleet. There was a deeply shiftless Holden and a Morris 1100 that drove as if it were Darth Vader's Starfighter at the end of *Star Wars*. However you tried to direct it, it would spiral off out of control deep into space. Dad had a stoic ute for a while that had a horn that sounded like an emu. In fact, the ute did its fair share of shopping centre tours. On a long trip to Pacific Fair where 'Each Shopping Day is a Holiday' Mum decided to play 'Guess that tune' on the emu-horn to pass the time. She got lots of angry waves, especially when she tried to toot 'Blue Hawaii'.

One day Dad told us none of the usual fleet was to be used as he was going to borrow Dean Martin's new Falcon 500. The news spread like wildfire throughout the house. 'Yes, too right – old Deano is lending us his car and he's going to borrow the ute to take the boys to footy.'

I couldn't believe it. Dean Martin. Dean Martin from Telly. The grown-up who simply arsed around and smoked; the man who slid down poles, made bad movies that were funny;

and the man who was on all the records that Mum and Dad would dance to.

We would watch them from the shadows of the verandah as they would slip on 'Everybody Loves Somebody' and dance a slow waltz in the darkness of the backyard. As the tune played and Dean crooned they would drift in and out of the flickering beams of the old fluorescent light in the shed. Whenever the cane toads hopped in too close, Dad would gently kick them aside. Just near the end, as Deano's voice went all warm and low, Dad would kiss Mum softly on the lips.

Suddenly it all made sense – no wonder Dad liked Dean Martin so much – he was a mate! Maybe he even hired stuff from Dad. 'I didn't know Dean Martin lived in Redcliffe!' I cried.

'Yes, mate, he certainly does,' my father said.

'Does Jerry Lewis live here too?'

Dad laughed. 'Yes, old Jerry, eh? Yeah, he works at the council, sunshine, in the rates department. Lives out in Kippa-Ring. See him on the red bus all the time. Bloody fruit tingle, he is.'

I still couldn't quite believe it. My six-year-old brain was exhibiting its first faint fluttering of scepticism but it was Rhian who assured me we would soon find out if it was really Dean Martin or just some bad joke of my father's.

'How?' I asked with a whine.

'If it's a good car like a Torana,' she whispered, 'then it's probably true, but if it's some old Kombi or Datto then Dad's just bulling.'

·

223

The next day any lingering doubts vanished. Purring up the lane was, incredibly, a deep green Falcon 500 XT. Its V-8 growled and from the upstairs window where I was pasting a Captain Cook sticker from the 1770–1970 celebration school pack onto the wall, I could see Dad speaking to a stocky man with dark curly hair. It had to be Dean Martin. I yelled to my sister. 'He's not wearing his black suit!' But by the time we had run downstairs to see him, Deano had already left.

'He had to push off, sunshine,' my father said. 'They're running a bit short on time. Look at that bloody car.' He ran a hand over the gleaming duco.

And then another staggering realisation struck me. 'Is Dean Martin Vaughan's footy coach?'

'Too right he is…and he's doing all right to get a car like this.' I saw our reflections in the car's paintwork – we all looked short and fat and pumpkin-headed. Dad didn't say anything, and for a second he had an unhappy look on his face like he was looking at a cake he couldn't have, but it was only for a brief moment, and then he smiled his big smile and held my hand. 'C'mon, sunshine, let's go for a drive!'

Well, where do you go in a movie star's Falcon 500? Deception Bay of course, because there were no shopping centres open on a Sunday. We sat in unimagined comfort as we roared along Anzac Avenue, whizzing past the big pine trees that were planted in remembrance to the fallen soldiers.

'Do you think I look like Steve McQueen in *Bullitt*?' Dad said to Mum.

'You silly sod,' she giggled. 'But it's marvellous, it's so smooth.'

'Yeah, there're no gears, love. It's an automatic.' Dad sounded as if he had the motoring world at his fingertips. We had all been wondering why we hadn't heard the endless crunch of metal on metal when he shifted the gears. We'd thought for a minute that his driving might have been getting better. An automatic. Old Deano really lived the life of Reilly. We stopped on the only hill that had a view overlooking the mudflats and mangroves of Deception Bay and sat there in Dean Martin's car…for hours.

But it all went horribly pear-shaped. The car wouldn't start, or to be more accurate, my father couldn't start it. Somehow the Old Man had managed to stop the thing in 'Drive' and then he couldn't figure out why it wouldn't start again. The first twenty minutes were sort of funny.

'You've broken Dean Martin's car, Dad,' I said.

'Well, we can blame Jerry Lewis, can't we?'

'Doesn't he use the red bus?'

'Yeah, well, what's his other mate? Old Frank Sinatra, yeah, he bumped into us.'

'Does he live in Redcliffe too?'

'No, he just pops over from Sandgate… What is wrong with this bloody car…' He turned the ignition again. Nothing. 'Oh Christ.' His head sank.

It turned tense.

'All right,' yelled my father. 'Nobody…say…anything… Be QUIET!'

He tried the ignition and yet again nothing happened.

'We'll just listen to the radio for a bit,' said Mum. She turned a knob and miraculously Dean Martin's rich baritone warbled out of the tinny speaker. He sang a song called 'Too Many Chiefs and Not Enough Indians'.

'Dean Martin is going to be so cross with you, Dad,' said Corby.

'For Christ's sake, will you stop going on about Dean bloody Martin! He's got a lemon of a car and right now it's as useless as tits on a bull!'

'Oh, Colin,' Mum said.

'Just blame Jerry Lewis,' I offered.

That was it. My father exploded. 'What is wrong with you, you flat-headed banjo player? Will you shut up about Jerry Lewis…and shut up about Dean Martin too.' He shook his head. 'Trust a bloody Mexican from Woody Point.'

There, and I thought Dean Martin was Italian.

Dad turned to my mother. 'Switch the radio off, love, it's draining the battery.'

'But I've only just put it on.'

'It's these new cars, love.' He was clutching at straws but the radio was switched off. We sat in silence. He tried the ignition again. Nothing.

Then he decided he'd have a go at fixing it. Whenever my father tried to fix anything there was an element of danger… and excitement.

Even changing a light globe could turn into an opera. One night he managed to touch something when his finger was in the light socket and he shot across the room while emitting an ear-splitting scream that any off-key tenor would have been proud of. He landed in the corner, stood up and with a straight face said, 'Well, that cleaned the wax out of me ears!'

So sitting on the hill overlooking Deception Bay, Dad decided to stick his head under the bonnet and look at an engine about which he had no comprehension. After a few minutes he reappeared and wandered about, looking for something. He picked up a rock, disappeared under the bonnet again and tried banging things with it.

'Did you know otters use rocks to break open shellfish?' my mother said to nobody in particular as the noise of Dad's efforts grew increasingly disheartened. Finally they stopped altogether.

'Mum, let's play "name that tune" on the horn,' Corby said after a minute or two.

'All right, I think your father's away looking for something.' The banging had stopped and we all assumed that he had gone off in search of a bigger rock. 'I'll give you a hint: this one's a television theme.' And with that Mum launched into a thundering attack on the horn in manic bursts. No sooner had she started, the car gave an almighty heave, there was a shriek, a dull bong and a scream of 'Holy mother of Christ! My bloody head!' Dad hadn't gone looking for a rock at all. He had slid in underneath the car and had copped the full force of the horn and the thickness of the chassis. We stared at him as he appeared from under the Falcon, clutching his head.

'I'm so sorry, Colin, I thought you'd gone off to find a bigger rock!'

'Bloody hell, Riss, you had to go and do "Hawaii Five-O", didn't you... Oh crikey. Are my ears bleeding?'

We tried not to laugh, but what could we do? My father started first and soon we were all in tears. Then without warning, he strode off up the road. He was gone around twenty minutes, and when he finally returned he had an enormous red egg of a lump on his forehead. He got slowly into the car, grasped the column shift and pointed the gear to 'Park'. He turned on the ignition and it purred into life. 'Bloody automatics,' he grumbled.

'Where'd you go?' asked Mum.

'Up the road to the phone booth by the shop. Rang Peter about his bloody car. You can't stop in "Drive"; it won't start.'

'Peter? Who's Peter?' I asked.

My father swivelled his red egg around to me and spoke very clearly. 'Peter Martin owns this car. He's a Mexican bloke who lives in Woody Point and his nickname is Dean. Dean Martin. Peter Martin. Dean Martin does not own this car; Peter Martin does.'

The car hummed and we sat in silence.

'Ripped off,' said Rhian.

'Yes, love,' answered my father. 'But never mind. I'm sure if Dean Martin owned a car, it'd be just like this one.'

We drove off and my mother squeezed Dad's arm. 'You look much nicer than Steve McQueen, Col.'

'Well, thank you, Riss. I do all my own stunts too.' He nudged Mum with his elbow. 'And I think I've found a nice bit of land for Rita. Up there in the window of the shop there's a notice.'

Two weeks later Aunty Rita bought a block of land at Deception Bay. In thanks she gave Dad a bottle of Scotch.

And a new Dean Martin record.

Aunty Rita was happy with the land because it was a fair size and like most of the Bay was still prime bush scrub. She liked having her own little parcel of the bush because she was a relief dairy farmer from way back, and would manage farms when the owner was away or unable to work. She never married and for a while lived with her mother. Nanna didn't think much of small children and took an instant dislike to me. I was tall and gangly, noisy and clumsy. She referred to me as 'The stupid one who makes the awful faces'.

Aunty Rita would just laugh and rumble. 'He's a dreadful boy but he'll grow into himself, eventually.'

After Nanna died Aunty Rita shared her little house and farm with several mad dogs and several rather pleasant cows. She'd hand-milk them. When she'd come to visit us in Redcliffe, which was often, she'd bring fresh milk in old wine flagons, chocolates and treats and gossip from the Bay. She loved a cigarette and a whisky and was always rubbing Rid insect repellent onto herself, for the mossies were evil out there on the Bay. To this day I associate three unmistakable scents with my Aunty Rita: cigarettes, Dewar's and Rid, and her scents remind me of her laughter.

She loved laughing and took pleasure in a joke or two. 'Nothing too blue, just a bit of innuendo.' Whenever we went to stay with her we'd delight in her collection of 'naughty' postcards and her semi-saucy tales of farm life. She'd wander about the house chuckling and giving little kisses to her pet galah named Cocky, who spent most of his time sitting on top of his cage. At night he would clamber in to go to sleep. Whenever I tried to give him a scratch or a kiss he would inevitably take a piece out of whatever part of my body was being offered with his murderous beak. 'Oh you've got to be careful how you kiss a cocky!' Aunty Rita would say with a wink. She also fed a family of magpies from her kitchen window.

'Hello, my darlings…whose a hungry boy then,' she'd say and would then gently drop tiny pieces of meat into open beaks. They would sit on the sink and sing to her.

I walked down the hallway of the hospital and the magpie's call was replaced by the hum of the air-conditioning. I waited in a cubicle outside the room where Aunty Rita was being treated. A tiny, neat doctor with kind eyes and an English accent came in, shook my hand and sat down beside me. He was the intensive care specialist.

'Your aunt has, we believe, suffered a severe stroke. We're not certain of the extent but it's caused a massive amount of damage. She's breathing with the aid of a ventilator.'

'Right,' I said. He looked at me.

'Right,' I said again. 'Should I be making telephone calls?'
The doctor nodded. 'I think that would be best.'

I went home and found my mother reading a story to my
children. She looked up and I told her what the doctor had
said. She put the book down and kissed my daughter on top
of her head. 'I'll go fix the beds up then,' she said.

The house was about to be full again. And we would wander
up to the hospital and wait by a bedside...again.

It had been a while since the house on the battleaxe block
had seen so many people. When I finished high school, I
packed my bags and went off to university, leaving Mum and
Dad and the dog to have the run of the place. Each Christmas
nearly all of us would drift back, but for most of the year my
parents were just voices down the telephone line. Mum would
pass on gossip from the town, what the senior cits were up
to next door, what she and Aunty Rita were up to with the
craft ladies at the pensioner hall, how the Church had
deconsecrated the *Brady Bunch* chapel, or how somebody had
lost a game of rugby for Redcliffe. How they had a great week
because the rubbish pick-ups were good. Then she'd put the
dog on. I'd hear some snuffling and some encouraging coos
from my mother to the dog, coaxing him to 'Sing to William'.
The dog would then howl or bark down the line. After the
dog Mum would stick my father on.

'How you going? You right?' he'd ask.

'Yeah, how about you?'

'Fine. I'm fine. You making money?'

'Doing all right.'

'Right then. Look after yourself. Here's your mother to say goodbye.'

As my father grew closer to retiring age he divested himself of his beloved trestles and cement mixers and sanders and the rest of his hire equipment. He sold the business to his friend Doug Hamilton but he kept his truck. Although he had to paint over the signs on the doors because the name belonged to Dougie now. He could still do the odd rubbish job.

One night there was a phone call from Mum. She didn't put the dog on or pass on any gossip about her and Rita and the craft ladies. She didn't even tell me who had lost what game and who had been up before the courts on general misdemeanours.

'It's your father. He's a bit crook.'

'What's up with him?'

'Oh...wait.' I could hear my mother talking to him in a muffled voice. 'Well, do you want to tell him? Why don't you tell him?' She turned her voice back to me. 'Here he is.'

'How you going?' My father's voice sounded much like it always did.

'Good,' I said. 'How you travelling?'

'Oh, you know... I've just got a touch of Old Timer's Disease...'

'Colin!' I heard my mother say in the background.

'Yeah,' said my father. 'The doctor told me I've got Alzheimer's disease, son.'

'Right,' I said.

'Yeah,' he said, and as an afterthought…'Making any money?'

'I'm doing all right,' I told him.

'Right then, here's your mother.'

Mum told me he'd been a bit odd for a while.

'What's "a while"?'

'Oh, six months or so. I tried to get him to go to the doctor but you know…he never liked going…' There was silence. 'It's not been much fun…he'd be up in the middle of the night getting cross with himself, going for walks along the beach at all hours. I just thought it was because he was retiring…like a little crisis… I didn't know…poor old sod. Will we see you at Christmas?'

That Christmas we all came home. I walked up the lane from the taxi and saw my father in the front yard. He was pushing a red carpet sweeper across the couch grass.

'Dad,' I called out to him.

'Hello, sunshine.' He looked up and smiled.

'What are you doing?'

'Trimming the lawn.'

I laughed. 'Dad, that's a carpet sweeper.'

His face broke into the most beautiful smile.

'Good job I didn't try and do the carpets then!'

We both laughed and went inside.

Over the next couple of weeks I took him down to the beach with my brother and sisters. He was still a big man physically but he would roam in his conversations and meander in his thoughts quite often. He would start a story but it would have no direction, and would segue into a recurring tale about a baby with no milk. He was like this throughout Christmas. Muttering something and then saying clearly, 'There's no milk for the baby.' Mum said he was drifting. He still knew who we were but the sense that something was dying was reflected in the house that Christmas. It was grey and oddly lifeless.

The family got together one breakfast and tried to decide what to do with him.

'Well, he's not going anywhere else but here,' my mother stated definitely.

'You'll need help,' said Corby.

'I don't want strangers looking after him, he wouldn't like it. I'll be right, he's my husband.'

That was the end of the matter. We agreed that we'd try to come up and see them more often.

Later that year at Vaughan's wedding, my father looked like a ghost. Vaughan had watched him creak off the bus that he and Mum and Aunty Rita had all caught down to Sydney. My father moved like a marionette and jerkily waved his hands at us. My brother turned to me. 'Thunderbirds are go.' It was hard not to laugh and I think that was because it was too easy to cry.

At the reception, when Mum and Dad wandered around the dance floor for the bridal waltz, great tears rolled down Aunty Rita's cheeks. 'Of all the people who it had to happen to.' She puffed on a fag and sipped her Dewar's.

Slowly the house began to shrink. My mother became Dad's sole carer and her sole concern became my father. As he became more frail and sick, the house seemed to ail with him. It smelt like an old man's house. Mum bathed and fed him, took him to the clinic and to keep him happy would take him out in his truck to do the odd rubbish collection job. She would heave great mounds of vegetation onto the back of the truck and drive it to the dump while Dad would hover about picking up the odd leaf and twig. Mum said he enjoyed these outings.

It was important to keep an eye on him. He loved to go wandering. Mum was worried that some harm would come to him. But Aunty Rita told her she needn't worry. Other people remembered the man he had been, and would look out for him. With his name, address and telephone number sewn into his clothes and underpants he would skive off as soon as he'd taken his afternoon medicine. One day he disappeared for hours. Mum rang Aunty Rita and the two of them tried to find him. Mum was about to ring the police, she was beside herself. Then the phone rang and kept ringing with different callers all afternoon. My father had gone wandering and somehow had followed his old door-knocking route from when he was standing for the elections. People would answer the door, remember him and so listen to him and make sure he was all right, then ring my mother to let her know. My father was delivered home just on dusk, led up the driveway by an elderly woman. 'Here he is,' she said to Mum. 'All safe and sound.'

My mother took her husband's hand. As she helped him walk towards the house, the older woman who had brought him home said, 'I never voted for him in those elections, but I always looked forward to him knocking on the door. He always laughed so much… I wish I had.'

It was late at night, sitting with them, that I could see how much Mum had lost. By now my father had no idea who I was and had almost completely forgotten about his family. My father couldn't remember to forget anymore. Where he was I had no idea. He wanted to go home, he said. Even when he stood in the living room of the house he had built, he turned to me.

'I'll give you twenty dollars if you take me home.'

'You are home, Dad.'

'Twenty dollars.'

'You are home, you silly old sod.'

He looked around slowly with his milky eyes. 'You're joking me.'

'No, I'm not joking you.'

'Do I know you?'

'I'm your son… you taught me to gargle.'

'He's your son,' chorused my mother. 'Who else would he be?'

'You're joking me.' He sat in his recliner and leant back into his past. Half-asleep he speaks to someone, somewhere about something that nobody in the house could understand.

We only hear raspy mutterings. Dribble stains mark the space on the recliner between his legs.

'Oh Christ, he's dribbling again,' Mum said. 'Colin, you're dribbling, dear.'

'Hello,' said Dad.

'He doesn't know he does it,' she said, looking at me fiercely.

'I know, Mum,' I say softly.

She turned back to him. 'Come on, Colin, it's time for your pill.'

He stared at her. He opens his mouth, then shuts it. 'You're trying to poison me.'

My mother closes her eyes. 'Take your pill.'

'These things are killing me.'

'Take your pill,' says my mother. 'For Christ's sake, take your pill.'

'Don't give me orders.' He glowered at her.

'Swallow it; and don't hide it under your tongue. Wash it down with this. Colin. Drink. Drink the water.'

As she speaks to him he smiles, visibly softening. 'I like a lolly...what's in there?' He gives Mum a kiss on her cheek.

'Goodnight, Dad.'

'Hello.'

'Goodnight.'

'Bye-bye...' He looks at me and then to Mum, then back to me. 'Are you living here?'

'No, I don't live here. I'm just staying for a little while.'

'You're staying?'

'He's staying just for a little while,' Mum said softly.

'You want to watch him…' Dad whispered to her, and then after a thought, 'Hide the tin.'

'Colin, he's your son.'

'Where?' His voice trembles.

'He's your son, William.'

'You're joking me.'

And then she led him up the dancers to bed.

In the backyard one morning, just before leaving, I tried to tell him I loved him. I sat with him and held his hand. I tried but I couldn't. He had no idea who I was. So we sat holding hands, with me sobbing. And my father telling me in his wispy voice, 'Don't worry, mate, you'll be right. We'll get you home.' He called to my mother. 'I think this fella's a bit upset. I think he's missed his bus.'

'Well, we'll see what we can do for him. We'll get him on home.'

The sun was very hot and Dad was wearing one of his old cloth hats. I got up to go. 'Well, I'll see you then.' I gave Mum a kiss. I looked at Dad and nodded.

He nodded back and then waved to me, an old man's wave, his index finger falling from his forehead and pointing out towards me. 'Well played, big fella. Ripsnorter!' my father said. 'Save ya pennies and we'll get you home.'

They were the last words he ever said to me.

Phone calls would come from my Aunty Rita and my mum. They would pass on the news that Dad was becoming increasingly weaker. He was diagnosed with Parkinson's and then to top it off, cancer.

'The poor old bugger's a real hamburger with the lot,' said Aunty Rita one phone call.

Then my mother rang and after putting the dog on told me that she had rung the family in order of oldest to youngest and so that was why I was the last to hear. 'I've been talking to a doctor at the hospital,' she said. 'And he seemed to think it would be a good idea if you were to come home for a little bit... Dad's on his way out.'

We all came back to the house on the battleaxe block. To wait. To wait for our father to die. He lay in a bed in the palliative care ward, grey and shrunken. His head turned towards the ceiling, his mouth open. A nurse would sometimes come and clear his throat with a suction hose. His eyes would only occasionally flicker in response. One of us was always with him. Throughout the hours, just to sit and wait with him.

It must have been easy for the hospital staff to tell which of us had been sitting with him. Each of us had our own way of passing the time with him. Rhian would put some soft flute or harp music on and then light aromatherapy candles. Sometimes she would rub some oils into Dad's temple or forehead. If Mum or Aunty Rita had visited, Dad's breath would smell slightly of Scotch. They would carefully give him a few wee drams to keep him going. Laurie would replace Rhian's harp music with Frank Sinatra or Tony Bennett and give Dad another nip of whisky. Vaughan and I would smell of whatever lolly or food we had just eaten. If there was the scent of chewy in the air it was a sign that Corby had visited.

We waited with him for over a week.

He felt cold. I heard him breathing but he felt cold. What was there left in him that was my father? His body was a vessel that had foundered on the rocks of time and sickness. I looked at his thinning hair and held his hands. They felt so slight. I could see the veins through his translucent skin. His skin had always been so brown.

'Are you cold, Dad?' I asked him. 'Is it the cold that makes you forget?'

To remember is painful, but surely to forget is worse. Is that what the end was? To simply forget. It would be painless to be sure, to gently slip away and let the cold make you forget. All those stories. All those people, locked up in his memory and then they slowly died as he forgot. As I looked at my father I realised I knew little of what he had been before I was old enough to remember him, and now I would never hear him tell me.

A burly wardsman covered in tattoos came in. He gently flipped my father over. 'I can remember your old man throwing those big trestles on the back of his truck,' he said. 'All by himself. Now I can flip him over with one hand.'

'Life,' I said to him, 'is so fucking unfair sometimes.' My words drifted off into the ward.

The wardsman looked at me. 'Oh well, we've all got to fall off the perch somehow.' He patted me on the shoulder and walked off back down the corridor.

And so it was that as I sat with him, I found myself thinking less about him. I found myself feeling a little less each time I looked towards him. And without knowing it I was feeling a bit more cold. I told myself that I had said goodbye to my father a long time before.

A few nights later, while I sat by his bedside flipping through a book, I heard some voices. Old men's voices. Three of them came shuffling into the room.

'Hello,' one of them said to me. Another nodded.

And the third said, 'How'd you be?'

'Good,' I replied. 'Good.'

One was wearing a trilby hat and carrying a plastic shopping bag. It rustled in his hands as he clicked his teeth. 'You'd be the youngest, then,' he said.

I nodded.

'Righto, then. Righto.' He breathed out a long sigh and smiled. 'Like a bit of time with your dad. Do you mind?'

'Sure, sure,' I said and went out to the kitchen area to make a cup of tea. I could hear them rattling around in my father's room, their mutterings deep and chesty.

'Now, you brought everything, did you?'

'Yes, here we go.'

'Right then.'

'Wait a tick.'

'New specs?'

'Yes…got them from the Indian chappy in Kippa-Ring.'

'Oh yes.'

'Yep, there a bit shiny and they slip off a little –'

'Use the old ones then.'

'You don't really need ya glasses, do ya?'

'Well no, I don't suppose I do.'

'Right then.'

'Here we go.'

I walked back to the edge of the room and peeped in through the doorway. The three old men milled around my father.

'Righto then.'

Some teeth clicked. A cough. One of the old men scratched his forearm slowly. The man in the trilby hat took it off and ran his hand through his grey hair.

'Righto then,' he said again.

The three of them stood stock-still and all that I heard was my father. The silence seemed to stretch forever, and softly they murmured together, 'Lest we forget.'

Then they slowly packed up their bits and pieces and waddled out. I walked down the hallway. One of them stopped at the doorway, looked back at Dad for a while and then gently waved his hand. 'Ta ta, mate.'

As they drifted past me, the taller one tipped his trilby hat and said to me, 'Be seeing you, then.'

I nodded. Whenever I talk to old men I seem to nod a lot. I wondered why that was so. Perhaps they had earned the right to use fewer words.

I went back into Dad's room and held his hands. They no longer felt cold. He had sunken into himself and his skin was sallow and almost transparent. But he wasn't a husk. He was still my old man. I held his hands tighter and remembered how big and brown and gentle they'd been. I laughed. 'Sorry, Dad. Sorry.' I sat down and flipped through my book with one hand, and with the other I held Dad's hand.

The books in the ward library were an odd collection. Old paperbacks by authors such as Alistair Maclean, Hammond Innes and Wilbur Smith. Real pipe-smoking man's man old adventure stories about mountain climbers and big game hunters, and renegade soldiers of fortune on suicide missions. There were old pulp magazines with star diets and divorces and operations and romances and spats. Out-of-date Chinese horoscopes, I read my father's out to him.

'It says here, Dad, that you've got to take time to consolidate for the future. Put off all thoughts of travel and don't enter into new business arrangements.' My father rasped away.

There was an old show guide with my sister's name in it for winning a cooking prize. It was all reassuringly similar to the bookshelves at my parents' home. The other choices were Mills & Boon, Barbara Cartland and a Harold Robbins novel called *The Betsy*.

I remembered *The Betsy* from my time at drama school. I had volunteered to go to a local nursing home because someone there thought it would be a nice idea if the elderly occupants had someone come to read to them.

I found myself sitting in a common area surrounded by about six or seven old ladies. Most of them had poor eyesight and one wore Coke-bottle glasses. The women had to be manoeuvred into a semi-circle around me. I started with

A Tale of Two Cities and then rather oddly, *Heidi*. The books were selected by the staff, so someone had a nice sense of humour. The old ladies would snore, dribble and fart away the afternoons while I droned on thinking I sounded wonderful and mellifluous.

I was halfway through *Heidi* when a lady named May asked me to stop reading. 'It's very nice, dear, but it's a little boring. Would you mind reading this one?' Her skinny arm held out a chunky paperback and her hand trembled ever so slightly. It was *The Betsy*. 'Just read the bits that are marked,' she said.

I shrugged and opened the book to the first of the pages that had been marked by neat squares of paper sticky-taped to the page. The girls had obviously done their homework. Now, I'd never read Harold Robbins, and I haven't since. But I'm sure *The Betsy* was one of his finest. In short, the scene involved sex, and lots of it: an older man with powerful hands and an enormous blood-engorged member (I'm quoting Harold here) was having his way with a French maid with huge breasts who was little more than half his age. '*Mon Dieu, mon Dieu,* you're breaking me in two!' gasped the French maid. I looked up to see my semi-circle of eighty-year-olds cackling and waving their hankies.

'Oh dear,' wheezed May, 'he's got a real kidney-belter, hasn't he?' She giggled and asked me to read it again. I did so. And again and again that afternoon.

I looked at *The Betsy* for a moment and considered reading it to Dad but decided against it. Just then my sister Laurie came in. She had spent the most time with Mum and Dad since my father had been ill.

'How is he?' she asked.

'Much the same.'

She glanced at the copy of *The Betsy* I was holding. 'What are you reading that for?'

'I'm not. I was looking through the shelves.' I pointed to the bookcase.

We talked about books and laughed at the convoluted plotlines.

She looked at Dad. 'Well, he's lived a life,' she said. 'Had his share of drama and crazy plotlines.'

'He's taking his time.'

'He'll go when he's ready.'

'"There's no milk for the baby." Remember how he used to say that?'

Laurie nodded. 'I think it was something to do with the war; something he saw once.' She told me that at the end of World War II Dad had marched into Belsen as a member of the liberating army. Amid all the horror, he saw a bedraggled woman in the camp, on the verge of dying, manage to drag herself over to a big soldier, a paratrooper. In her arms was a ragged bundle. She gave it to the soldier. 'My baby, my baby needs milk, please,' she said in broken English.

The big soldier took the tiny bundle into his arms. The baby had been dead for days, perhaps it had never breathed. 'Righto then,' he said, knowing there was no milk. Even so he cradled the child and said softly, 'Some milk, get some milk for the baby.'

'Jesus wept,' I said.

'Yeah,' said Laurie. 'Dad's lived a life all right.'

The next day I left. I had to go to work.

A few days later in the middle of the night it came. The phone call.

'He's gone,' said Rhian. 'He's just gone now.'

All that waiting by the bedside, and now it was happening again. It was over ten years since my father had died. It seemed like a moment and then it seemed like an age. Just before my aunt had suffered her stroke my daughter had a birthday. My daughter – I'd married and had children since my father had died. In the intensive care ward I thought of that birthday. I thought of the Fairy Queen.

14

When I was a boy, birthday parties consisted of paper hats, chocolate crackles and a maybe a bottle of Tristam's sarsaparilla. There was the excitement of seeing one of the 'good' bedsheets ballooning down upon the table to act as a tablecloth for a feast, and the coveted envelope from Nanna which would always be held to the light to determine the size of the note inside. Green for two dollars and joy of joys purple for five!

My daughter's party wasn't held at home and the Fairy Queen was late. Little girls milled around the legs of their parents. The parents murmured words to the little girls. Words intended to soothe and calm their concerns. 'It won't be long. I'm sure it won't be long.'

Where was the bloody Fairy Queen? I tried to remain calm and proclaim in a voice designed to be reassuring but unfortunately I came across as a little shrill and forced, 'I'll just pop out and rustle up the Fairy Queen.'

I ran through the fairy cave and into a waiting room then onto a kitchenette. Nobody. Mournful words from a forty-year-old man echoed off the lino, 'Hello, is the Fairy Queen here?'

I opened the door onto a walkway leading down to the bottom of a yard, and there she was, the Fairy Queen. Hurrying up the path, sucking like a vacuum cleaner on a cigarette that was quickly evaporating and then rushing out of her nostrils.

'I haven't had a smoke for six months,' she told me. 'Had a party of boys through just before. They always get you going.'

She wafted past me, smoke streaming from her like a special-effects machine from the old *Countdown* days. It's a glam rock revival. She picked up her wand, squirted a breath freshener down her throat. There was booming music and the Fairy Queen announced that she had arrived for the birthday meeting of Fairy Princesses. Little girls' voices screamed in delight.

Renne, the Fairy Queen's offsider who was wearing an eye-patch, winked at me with her one good eye, 'What a way to make a living, eh? Better see to the sausy rolls.'

What a way to make a living indeed. Providing a birthday party service to children. Across the nation this is how a large number of parents celebrate their children's birthday. They pay people to entertain and organise a party. The fairy cave is quite modest really. An old shop that is bordered by a butcher's on one side and a hardware store on the other. The insides have been transformed into a fairy cave for girls and a castle and adventure cave for boys. Most of the time it's a mixture of both. To me it is a scene of madness and chaos.

There are so many places and people who provide these niche services. I think what my father and Aunty Rita would have made of it all. Occupations that are performed by smiling adults in franchised uniforms, occupations that I used to do as a way of earning pocket money. Now people feed their families with them.

Services like dog washing, lawn mowing, car washing, house cleaning, dog walking and, yes, birthday parties.

I once tried to hire a clown for my son's birthday. A party at home. 'Beppo' was recommended by a friend. I phoned Beppo and he said he could maybe squeeze me in but that I really should have organised things sooner. I was going off Beppo. I went off him completely when I found out that he wanted two hundred dollars for his show. 'Fire-eating included.'

I didn't need to rent a clown for my son. He already had one...his father. I could do magic; well, no I couldn't, but I could pretend. And how hard could it be to breathe fire? Just spit a bit of methylated spirits on a match and you're away. So with the help of our dog, Doug, I began the show. Ten eight-year-old boys and a few little girls stared at me as I announced that I was going to breathe fire and do magic. The children were less than impressed.

I lit my torch, which was an old nappy wrapped around the handle of a broken tennis racquet, took a sip of metho and spat. Nothing happened and so I took a bigger swig and slagged it forth.

I erupted into a ball of flame. It was spectacular.

The kids cheered. I saluted them. My torch was still aflame. My hair caught on fire and the kids heard a few magic words dropped as they went wild. But I wasn't finished yet. For some reason, don't ask me why, I thought it would be funny if Doug were to shoot streams of poo from his bum. I really don't know why this counts as magic but the only excuse I can give is that my brain was singed. The sad thing is that it was premeditated. I had filled surgical gloves with spaghetti and meatballs from a tin and had strapped them to a perplexed but loyal Doug. I placed him on my still-smouldering magic table and squeezed the glove's contents across the lawn and onto a plate that was marked as a target. The audience went crazy.

Let's see Beppo top that. I was on fire, literally and figuratively. I went over to the plate and held it before my smoking face. 'Good enough to eat!' I yelled like a maniac. The kids laughed. I ate a meatball.

There was silence.

Then they started screaming so I had to quickly explain the magic trick. I think the kids understood. I hoped they never told their parents.

A few weeks later Mum, my daughter and I were watching the video of the party. When it came to the part where I tried to breathe fire and ignited my hair, Mum gave me a withering look.

'What?' I said.

'You're a bloody idiot.' She looked back at the screen. 'But your father would have been proud of you, dear, that's something right out of his book.'

I smiled.

That was two years ago. Now I'm so much wiser. The Fairy Queen could do the magic. And the kids loved it, a real treat. At the end of our allotted two hours we said goodbye. The fairy cave was a mess.

One little girl who has been a friend of my daughter for years came to say goodbye and thank you. She walked arm-in-arm with my daughter.

I laughed with her mum as we agreed that it's a much better way to have a birthday party, here at the fairy cave. 'I think they're happier here, they don't really notice,' I said.

Her little girl smiled up at me. She whispered to my daughter and then my girl laughed. 'Thank you for my party, Daddy,' she said. 'But next year can you and Dougie do magic for us? In our backyard?'

I groaned and said we'll see.

Next year is a long time away. But even though it's convenient I don't want to wish her birthdays away and I know that next year, even though the fairy cave is fun, it'll be chocolate crackles and magic with Doug and Dad underneath the plum tree.

As I stood in the intensive care ward there was something there for me to grasp as I remembered those birthdays. I looked at Aunty Rita and I wished there were something about the passing of time and the generations that would make things seem clearer. Perhaps it's not that things would be clearer, perhaps it's that things could be accepted. There is something, I know that much, but it is something that eludes me.

The neat English doctor told us that we wouldn't have to wait long. It would only be a matter of days, he thought. I looked at Aunty Rita's face sagging and bloated. It looked lifeless. The night before she'd had the stroke we'd all been out to dinner at a restaurant called The Fish Bowl and she told us one of her favourite stories. She had been working as a relief dairy farmer in the Hunter Valley. The farmer was an old friend of hers who had broken his arm when he fell while trying to bring the cows in for milking and so Aunty Rita had taken over the farm for a month.

At first nothing much happened. The routine of the farm ground on. But the farmer grew bored and decided to have a night out. Later, in the wee hours, Aunty Rita heard a strange moaning coming from one of the sheds (she was a chronic light sleeper). She thought at first it might have been an animal. As the muffled moans continued, stopping and starting, she decided to investigate and grabbed a torch and the farm rifle. It had started raining but she could still hear the moaning over the pitter-patter on the tin roofs. She walked slowly across the yards to the closest shed and as she neared the door she realised the cries were human.

'I slowly opened the door, the rain trickling down my back – I was in my pyjamas and had no idea what I was going to find. The light in that shed didn't work, so I squeezed the torch and raised my rifle to get a bead on whatever it was that was in there.' At this point she broke into guffaws. 'Get a bead, get a bloody bead. I had no idea what I was doing! But my God, when I shone the torch, my God! Well, you've never seen anything like it.' She paused and had a sip of her gin and tonic and picked at something in her teeth. 'I shone the torch and as I did I saw this thing leap up and then crouch back down. It was silly bloody Lionel. He'd gone and had too much to drink and waltzed into the wrong shed thinking it was the outhouse. There was a crack of thunder. I shone the torch and as I did I saw this thing leap up and crouch back down.' Aunty Rita lowered her voice and roared, 'Oh my balls! Oh my bloody BAAAAAALLLS!'

She cackled with laughter. 'Lionel thought he was on the toilet but he'd sat on a paling bucket. Every time he tried to get up he'd stand on the paling bucket lever and that would shut the squeezing mechanism over his balls. His *balls*!' She was beside herself and people around her were in fits. She wiped away the tears. 'I tell you, they were the size of ruby red grapefruit!'

I stood looking at her amidst her tubes and machines, and laughed. She had been an outrageous woman. There in her little house she would train her bird-watching binoculars on her neighbours and see what was happening. Her farm was gradually surrounded by housing estates and as they crept ever closer she would have her favourite new surveillance targets.

'I tell you, I think there's something fishy going on in that brick house.' The fact that they were all brick houses seldom put a dent in Aunty Rita's reports. 'There's something definitely a little bit odd. Perhaps it's drugs! They eat a lot of pizzas, you know.'

It was in her little house that she had settled down early on a Sunday morning to eat a Drumstick ice-cream. She unwrapped it and was about to have a bite when she suffered her stroke.

Now she lay waiting to die while doctors ran tests and fiddled with her. I felt angry, waiting. Hospitals, I decided, were similar to airports: shiny places with fluorescent lighting, filled with people who are waiting. People behind desks smile and say that they are doing all they can, and would you like a hospitality card? One time, when I was stranded at Los Angeles airport, I was approached by a man in a maroon uniform. He had the biggest afro hairdo I had ever seen, one brown eye and one green one, and I'd say he was about half a chromosome off being an albino.

'Here, sir, would you like to take a hospitality card?' It was more of an order than a question. 'Sorry for your delay.'

My flight had been delayed six hours so I accepted the card gratefully, thinking it'd mean drinks in a bar or perhaps even a meal. But there was no bar name on the card; instead it informed me that I was entitled to a tour of the stars' homes. Jesus wept, I thought.

'William!'

I looked up to see an Australian theatre director I vaguely knew smiling at me. She was a long way from home. 'What are you doing in LA?' she cried. I sensed a very uncomfortable hour or two ahead.

I felt for the card in my hand. 'Well, I was going to have a drink but I'm just off to have a quick look at some real estate.'

'Reeeeeally?'

'Yep. Hooroo,' I said, waving goodbye and boarding the Quality Touring Company mini-bus. It was filled to the brim with eager-eyed tourists and I reckon I was the only one onboard who wasn't wearing a tracksuit, or as they call them in the States, 'leeeeeisure suits'. I was also the only one under the age of about fifty. And I'm positive I was the only one who wasn't on some pretty heavy prescription medication.

Our guide and 'good buddy' for the day was Dwayne. He introduced himself and assured us that we were going to have a real neat day and see some real nice houses that belonged to real famous people. 'Are we happy about that guys?' A few answered back.

'I can't hear you, guys. Are we *happy* about that?'

Everybody on the bus yelled back except me. I flinched. Audience participation on a bus tour. I looked around. Everyone nodded and laughed like muppets. I groaned.

Dwayne continued. 'I just want to let you know that we're waiting on a few of our friends before we head off. While we do that, I want to tell you a little about myself.' I looked out the window and saw two people staggering towards the bus. Dwayne coughed and had a sip of water. 'I'm a recovering alcoholic and a writer. I've been working on a story about a young man's search for what baseball's really all about. I want to assure you that I haven't touched a drink for over 254 days and I think that deserves a little applause.'

Some of the muppets clapped while others looked about uneasily.

'I would also like to point out that in the sleeve of the seat in front of you is a message from a great friend of mine, Jesus Christ.' Dwayne paused while he received more applause. 'Oh, thank you so much, from both of us.'

There was indeed a pamphlet in the seat pocket in front of me. It was like a *Watchtower* and reminded me of the man with the dark glasses who held slide shows in the Senior Citizens' Hall back in Redcliffe. The bus lurched as the two latecomers stepped down the aisle. They were a couple – an elderly, thin man who was the size of a pipe cleaner and a woman who was huge. She looked like the actor from *Whats Eating Gilbert Grape*. They sat down beside me. The woman smiled. The man sat breathing hard; his skin was very brown and very saggy. He gurgled as he breathed. He wore chequered shorts and a pink polo shirt; big aviator-style sunglasses and a baseball cap with a warship on the front. He chewed gum. His large partner was much younger than him and wore a bright yellow leisure suit and lots of jewellery. Her hair was big and curly.

We drove along in silence. Then Dwayne hit the brakes rather abruptly and there were a few squeals as a motorcyclist rode past. 'My apologies, guys. Just had a near miss there with our friend on a motorbike. You know we have a term for people on motorbikes here in LA; we call them organ donors.'

Most of the muppets laughed.

Then Dwayne had a neat idea. 'Now, I introduced myself to you guys so why don't we just do a little something to make the trip a little bit more friendly. Turn to the person next to you and introduce yourself.'

Mrs Gilbert Grape turned to me. 'Hello,' she said.

'Hello,' I replied.

She elbowed the old man beside her. He grunted. 'Oh, Emmett,' she said and sighed. 'My name's Barbara and this is my husband, Emm –'

She was cut off by her husband who sounded like Darth Vader. His voice was startling in its deepness. 'Ma name is Emmett Karl and this is my wife Barba-wa.' The way he said her name it sounded like 'Barbed Wire'.

The woman smiled at me. 'And we are saying hello to…?'

'Herod,' I said.

'Herod?' She didn't blink. 'Well, that's a nice name.' She elbowed Emmett Karl again. He grunted a low rumbling moan.

'Oh, Emmett,' she sighed.

Over the next three hours I learned that Emmett Karl and Barbed Wire were from Florida, had recently married and were on their honeymoon. I also learned that Emmett Karl was thirty years older than Barbed Wire.

We drove past a marina and Dwayne pointed out that this place was the harbour from the beginning of *Gilligans Island*. Cameras whirred and people muttered. Dwayne then pointed out an enormous white yacht. 'Now that big white motor yacht is the property of the famous movie actor and singer Mr John Travolta.'

Emmett Karl rumbled, 'God damned Scientologist creetin.'

Barbed Wire elbowed him. 'Oh Emmett.'

We drove up through Hollywood past some homes. Big homes. Dwayne asked us all to 'please respect the privacy of these folks, you know they're famous but they have feelings too.'

I was gobsmacked at this sensitivity from Dwayne. It seemed slightly out of place as a busload of celebrity-watching pervs readied their cameras. My head snapped up when suddenly Dwayne screamed like Captain Ahab upon seeing Moby Dick. 'There! There on the right! Nicolas Cage's house! There's somebody there, is it Nicolas? Nic?' Dwayne's words hung in the air.

A small man in a white floppy hat and carrying a bucket looked at us as we drove slowly past.

'No, no, no... maybe it's his gardener. You guys have driven past Nicolas Cage's gardener... maybe.' Dwayne's tone became pensive. 'You know these folks get a lot of help. They're rich, but are they happy? I wonder if they're as happy as that gardener. Makes you think.'

It was completely insane.

We drove past Ronald Reagan's house. 'He's been a little sick lately,' Dwayne said as if talking about a neighbour. We were then invited to look at a huge white building that was the home of Aaron Spelling. 'He has many famous friends. In fact, that's where Prince Charles of England stays when he's in town.'

'There's another reason to become a republic,' I said to myself.

'You don't like royalty?' asked Barbed Wire. 'I think they are so romantic.'

'God damned parasites,' rumbled Emmett Karl.

Barbed Wire elbowed him so hard it sent his hat spinning off onto the floor. His hair was the colour of fresh bitumen and he wore it in a style that can only be described as the comb-over from hell. Barbed Wire saw me looking at her husband's do. 'Did it myself, Herod. I'm a hair stylist.' She lurched down and picked up Emmett Karl's cap, carefully flicked a few strands of hair on his brown scalp and then pulled the cap down over his head. 'Well, thank you, Barbara,' she said. And then answered herself, 'You're welcome, Emmett Karl.'

Emmett Karl growled. He sounded like Lurch from *The Addams Family*.

Dwayne stopped outside another monstrous house, but this one was old and crumbling. 'Look at this pool,' said Dwayne. 'It used to belong to a guy called Johnny Weissmuller. He was Tarzan for a little while and also Jungle Jim.'

I hummed a few bars of 'Tijuana Taxi' and imagined what a pool party fundraiser for the Labor Party would have been like at Johnny Weissmuller's. All Labor Party texta-coloured Jungle Jims yodelling with Johnny and eating devils on horseback.

The pool was immense; it drifted over three levels and was landscaped like a wild river. But time and neglect had taken their toll and as I looked at it I could have sworn it had been designed by the same mob who did the Cascades at Humpybong Creek.

It was empty and the concrete was chipping. Safety fences covered sections that looked dangerous. An empty house is just an empty building, but this one looked like a skeleton. A skeleton of what was left of a life.

'You know Johnny got very sick, had a lot of marriages and ended up going nuts in Acapulco. So who says that money and fame can't buy you happiness and a contented soul?' Dwayne was on some sort of fundamentalist mission.

'Jesus,' I muttered, shaking my head.

'That's right, Herod,' said Barbed Wire. 'He said that and a lot of good things besides.'

We drove away from Johnny Weissmuller's big pool and stopped outside an old cinema shaped like a Chinese temple. It must have been a big deal when it opened back in the 1930s but now it looked like your average suburban Chinese restaurant. Outside in the cement pavement was a collection of foot and handprints autographed by famous film stars. 'Wander around and see if you can find the name of your favourites,' said Dwayne. 'And you know what? Even though thousands of people want to see them, most of their names are just made up. They didn't use their real ones 'cause their real names weren't American enough.'

I looked at the names as I wandered in and out of the drifting leisure-suited pilgrims. They all clucked and muttered and took photos of themselves, pressing shutter buttons with arthritic hands.

'Oh look, there's Tyrone Power, he was so handsome,' Barbed Wire said.

'Who's Tyrone Power?'

'Oh, he was Zorro and Jesse James and oh, he was *so* handsome. And Shirley Temple; look how tiny her feet are!'

'Who the hell is Wallace Beery?'

'Oh, Emmett.'

Clark Gable, Claudette Colbert, Jane Russell and Jimmy Stewart – all stars Mum, Dad and Aunty Rita used to watch at the cinema when they were younger. All names that belonged, or according to Dwayne didn't belong, to people who were dead and gone. In fact, they were names of people who might have been wandering the arcades of Redcliffe for the amusement of myself and my mate Peter Bolton. I saw Spencer Tracy's name and could think only of his doppelgänger slapping up and down Comino's Arcade.

Perhaps it was because of this dual vision of movie stars and their Redcliffe manifestations, and the cement beneath my feet outlasting them both, that I looked at the footprints and the handprints and the scrawled handwriting and was struck by how transitory we all are. Actors and actresses who in life were just shadows of light on a movie screen must have had a good idea how fickle their fame was, but they had played along with the game and imprinted pieces of themselves in the footpath.

I was struck by those images of cave paintings, of outlines of hands in caves as far away as possible in time and place as these scribblings in lumpy cement. How elemental and basic it had seemed. How very human to leave an imprint, a mark of your existence. Not much separates us all, I thought.

Suddenly Emmett Karl exploded in a phlegmatic cough.

'Oh!' cried Barbed Wire. 'It's Rock Hudson!' Emmett Karl continued to hawk. 'He was so good looking and he was so good with Doris Day.'

'You know,' chipped in Dwayne, who'd been standing nearby, 'that wasn't her real name; her real name was some unpronounceable Polish word. Doris was her real name but not her surname and that's the one that counts.'

'He was in *McMillan and Wife* too, and in *Giant* and –' Barbed Wire was stopped by what sounded like a pistol shot. It was Emmett Karl spitting on Rock Hudson's star. 'God damned homosexual creetin,' he rumbled.

Nobody said anything. It was dry and dusty and the air smelt of smog. People stared at Emmett Karl's bile on the pavement.

'Did you ever see the movie where Rock Hudson uses a K-Tel bottle cutter?' I asked Emmett Karl for no particular reason.

He swung his emaciated frame towards me and I saw myself reflected in his black sunglasses. He breathed at me and I took that as a no.

'Too bad. It's supposed to be pretty good.' And with that, I walked around the corner. As I strode off I heard Barbed Wire almost sob, 'Oh, Emmett'.

The whole area was dirty and sand seemed to seep everywhere. I didn't know where I was going but I knew I wanted to get away from the Quality Touring Company. I wanted to go home. As I walked I looked down at the cement footpath. I looked down and saw a footprint and handprints. It was the message that I remember the most. Emblazoned around the corner from the movie stars' memorial was the message, 'I'm famous too! Fuck you all!! Trent '01.'

No, not much separates us all.

I looked at my Aunty Rita. The staff had told us to talk to the patients. 'They find it soothing,' a friendly nurse had said. I think all of us felt a little self-conscious talking to her. It wasn't like in the movies or on the telly, you couldn't just talk about your shopping. I stared at Aunty Rita, at her and her machines.

'I saw Tarzan's pool,' I began, 'but it was empty; broken.' I paused, then added, 'He went mad, down in Mexico, you know.' I suddenly felt so sad I nearly cried, but instead I let out a soft moan, like a tiny Tarzan call.

The nurse came back and said softly, 'Perhaps she just wants to go. Perhaps she'll be better off, she'll be at peace.'

'I don't know. She'll never feed her magpies and never walk on the mudflats at dusk and hear the wading birds sing. She'll never have another nip of Dewar's down amongst the scrub. And she'll never know what the people in the brick house are up to... Who's to say she'll be better off?'

The nurse smiled. 'You all came up here. It's nice to see someone so loved.'

I smiled back. 'I came up from Melbourne to go to a school reunion. And she had a stroke. The reunion's tomorrow night.'

I held Aunty Rita's swollen hand. 'She's easy to love. She made me laugh a lot.'

'I'm sorry,' said the nurse.

'Do you remember Doris Day?' I asked.

'No, I don't. Who was she…a friend?'

'No,' I said. 'She was just some Polish woman apparently. Her name's in cement.'

The next morning the two doctors looking after Aunty Rita asked us to gather in a briefing room. There was the neat little English man with the kind eyes and an abrasive languid doctor with thick glasses.

'Gee, there's a lot of you,' the languid doctor said.

We didn't reply.

The neat little English doctor took a deep breath and began his prepared speech. He must have delivered it a lot of times. 'What we have to question now is Rita's –' He paused and looked at us. 'Sorry, Aunty Rita's quality of life. She won't be the same person, she won't be able to breathe without the aid of the machines. What we're asking you to think about is letting nature take her course.'

It's odd how such a corny line, said so often in dodgy movies and TV shows, can have such a poetic ring.

'You want to switch the machines off,' said Mum evenly.

'I think you have to consider –'

Mum finished his sentence for him. 'Letting nature take her course.'

'She's suffered a massive, massive stroke,' said the languid doctor. 'Her brain has been damaged...damaged beyond repair. She would have felt no pain and in fact the last thing she was probably conscious of was thinking about how nice that ice-cream was going to be. Not a bad way to go.'

Mum laughed gently. The neat little doctor smiled.

'I like to think she got her first bite...that's the best part of an ice-cream,' he said.

My mother smiled and sat up very straight. 'All right. Let's let nature take her course.'

We gathered around Aunty Rita's bed and the English doctor started to unplug the machines. He was so solemn one of my sisters started to giggle. 'He looks like he's trying to set up Telly at Christmas,' she whispered to me. I snorted.

My brother reached his hand out to Mum and gently waved to her to come and stand closer. For a brief moment he looked uncannily like my father.

The ventilator was removed and for a short while Aunty Rita breathed on her own. I watched the life slip away from somebody who had known me since I was born. I thought about the smell of the early morning rain on her small parcel of bush; of how she would hold out her hands to catch the drops and how it would bead on her fingers. Of how she would laugh as she flicked the watery pellets at me.

Aunty Rita shuddered and Mum made a sound like a pigeon. A soft, sad little sound. 'Oh Rita,' she said. 'Safe journey.'

Aunty Rita's lips seemed to blow out as if she had just come back from a long, hot walk. Her face collapsed. And then. And then she died.

We made our way separately back to the house, some via the shops or by the beach; others, like me, along Humpybong Creek.

Later, as I sat with Mum, she gently patted my head. 'You might as well go off and have a nice catch-up at your reunion.' She closed her eyes and hummed an old tune. I gave her a kiss on her cheek.

15

The first person I ran into at my school reunion was a man who as a pimply teen had once offered me ten bucks to eat his spit. We were in the E Block toilets and I said I didn't think it was a good idea. He told me that I was a cat and a piker and that 'Even if you'd eaten me spit I wouldn't have given you the money.' Twenty years on, what on earth do you say to a person who would offer such a challenge? After a few moments of considered thought I came up with, 'How are you?'

What a promising start.

I'd told a friend that I was going to the reunion and she had looked aghast. Apparently the only people who went to these sorts of things were those who thought they were successful and wanted to rub their schoolpals' faces in it.

Was it really like that? I wasn't sure.

Whatever the case, I must admit I felt distinctly uncomfortable as I walked into the hall that night. And why wouldn't I? Suddenly seeing a roomful of people I hadn't seen for twenty years. A collection of people that I'd spent my adolescence with, day after day. I looked around, the room was filled with strangers; men and women just shy of middle age standing roughly together as one. I felt like a fool. I was on the verge of leaving when suddenly I recognised someone. He was a big bloke, wearing a deep blue jacket and designer glasses. I reckon he would have been described by Mum's friends as 'cutting a fine figure'.

'Grink!' I cried. As I walked over to him someone called my name and I turned to see the mighty Jeff White beaming down at me. He's a plumber nowadays and was the only bloke who'd come out over Christmas when Mum had an 'emergency'. Mum had told me to say a special hello to him. When I relayed Mum's message he became very professional. He shook his big friendly head and gave me a wink.

'Backed-up dunny over Christmas, mate, not good... Good to see ya mum eats well, though!' He boomed with laughter.

As I wandered around the hall, snippets of conversation flew up to me like pieces of jigsaw puzzles...

'After my first marriage...

'She has had it done...

'Always knew he'd get fat...

'She shot through, or was it him who pulled the plug...

'Then my second divorce cost me the business...

'You should, you should have a vasectomy...

'She's definitely had it done...

'Then we've just bought the investment units down the Coast...

'Definitely, a breast reduction...

'Three kids, yes...

'Still trying...

'Keep making the same mistake...

'Wayne McIvor was my first crush...

'God why did she do that?

'Nearly knocked me over...

'Died just on Christmas...

'In her SAAB...

'WAYNE was?

'Done very well for himself...

'Beetle isn't coming...

I saw our old footy captain, Shane Bowering, looking the spitting image of his father. As he spoke, I was transported to a time when we gathered under the goalposts and he quietly told us to watch our defence.

Shane filled me in on why Beetle wasn't coming. Apparently he had a pizza conference on and couldn't make it. Priorities, I guess, are priorities. Shane told me that Beetle was a bit of a pizza king these days down the coast. Sure enough, although the man himself couldn't come he'd arranged for his excellent pizzas to be delivered.

As the night wore on, stories were told, old flames were laughed at, photos of kids were swapped, and just like the twenty intervening years, time flew by too quickly. I chatted with people who I was really fond of, and found myself wondering why we hadn't kept in touch.

When I was told by a woman whom I liked at that moment as much as I did when we were both sixteen and laughing at a particularly entertainingly odious history teacher, that she had had a serious cancer scare, I felt ashamed. I hadn't known. But I felt I should have. I looked at Anne and tried to say something but she laughed and touched me on the arm and told me not to worry.

We've all drifted away...that's life.

The next day work called. I had to go back. I packed my bags and asked my son a favour. 'Can you go to Aunty Rita's funeral for me, mate, and say goodbye to her for both of us?'

He looked me straight in the eye and assured me that he would.

Vaughan gave me a lift to the airport and as we bumped up and down over Hayes Inlet I counted the pelicans perched on top of the light poles along Houghton Highway. There were fifteen of them. Sometimes they would drop poo on the cars as they whizzed beneath. As always, my brother's car radio was tuned to the local FM community radio station and the music they played seemed to have come straight from my parents' record collection. The disc jockey even sounded a bit like my father's friends used to sound.

'And that was the, uh, legend uh himself...there...eh... Old...um... Elvis, yes, old Elvis and his big song from... uh, oh, whenever it was..."In the Grotto". Yes eh?'

My brother and I laughed and shook our heads. After an ad about taxi driving being the occupation of the new millennium, the man on the radio played a song my father had liked. It was an old singer called Al Bowlly singing 'Whatever Happened to Love'. We listened to the song. Pelican poo splodged onto the bonnet while Al warbled his lovely old tune.

'It's good luck when a bird shits on you,' said my brother.

'It landed on the car, not us,' I said.

'Good luck for all of us – you, me and the car,' he said.

'It's a bugger I'm going to miss the funeral,' I said as the song played.

'Yeah.' Vaughan was quiet for a minute. 'Remember that little man from the funeral parlour at Dad's funeral?'

I laughed. 'Yeah.'

None of us could understand what the little man with the red face was trying to say. He wore a sombre suit and his hair slicked back, and I could see bits of dandruff flaking on his shoulder as I leant in towards him to hear him. I think he was trying to be respectful of the moment, but I couldn't hear a word he was saying. 'What is it, sorry?' I asked, squinting at him. 'You'll have to speak up a bit.'

He must have had only two positions on the volume dial because after a deep breath he went for broke. 'Would you like to view the body?' he boomed, his voice echoing around the cavernous crematorium like a penny dropped in a deep well.

I turned to the family. 'I think he might be trying to ask if we'd like to view the…to have a look at Dad.'

We weren't all that keen but then Rhian said that she would and so we all traipsed into the little ante-chamber. The man had turned the volume down and hovered about at the back.

'Oh, hello, Colin,' said Mum. She sounded like Dad had just walked through the door.

We looked at him for a few moments.

'You've given him one of *those* hats,' said my brother. Dad was wearing a tiny cloth cap.

'He liked them,' said Mum.

'Yeah, well he liked boiled onions too,' said Vaughan.

'Who's to say she didn't give him some of those as well?' my sister Laurie said.

My other sisters started to laugh.

'I might have, too,' said my mother.

'Maybe you should have put a Makita cap in there,' I said.

'Oh God, do you remember those bloody things?' said Mum. 'And his Robin Hood hats!'

We laughed.

Mum bent down and gave him a kiss. 'Oh Christ, he's like a plucked chook.'

'Mum!'

'Well…'

'Oh, Col,' said Corby.

'Bye-bye, Dad,' said Rhian.

'So long, Col,' said Laurie.

We laughed a bit more and then my brother said, 'Righto then.'

'Night night, Chubbles,' Mum said softly.

We went back outside to the chapel and had the service. The priest said some words.

'Colin will go now to meet his maker, meet him on his own terms, for that is the sort of man he was and I think I know that the welcome for him will be warm, for another carpenter has entered the Kingdom of Heaven. A man who was never afraid to let the world know he was alive is always welcomed wherever he may journey.'

Everyone laughed, the priest included, and the chapel was filled with the sounds of life.

'Never be afraid to let the world know you're alive,' my father had always said.

They played a few songs that he and Mum used to dance to and then somebody pressed a switch and they cremated him. As we turned to go, Al Bowlly crooned 'Love is the Greatest Thing'.

Mum selected two plots in the rose garden at the Redcliffe cemetery: one for her and one for Dad.

Many Christmases later when the house on the battleaxe block was once again full to the brink, Vaughan and I decided we'd take the kids out early one morning so our wives could get some peace. It was either a trip to the beach or to Gilligan's lagoon. 'On no accounts,' said my sister-in-law, were we to 'nick off to McDonald's.'

My brother rolled his eyes and nodded. It was an overcast day and the sky was threatening to drizzle. We drove aimlessly about in the car.

'Jesus, where can we take them?' Vaughan said.

I turned to the kids. 'You want to go see the old wreck at Woody Point?'

Five little faces looked back at me.

'We're going there this arvo, Uncle Bill,' said one of my nieces.

'To chase the little blue crabs,' added my daughter.

'Yeah, Uncle Bill,' said my brother.

'Can we get the boat and go fishing?' asked my son.

'No mate, that's tomorrow,' said my brother.

'Can we go…can we go…'

'Come on, we'll go see your Pop.'

'What?' I said.

'We'll go see his grave, Uncle Bill,' said my brother.

'Yeah? You know I've never been there,' I said.

'Oh, Uncle Bill,' my brother said in an admonishing tone. Then he added, 'Neither have I.'

We wandered around the cemetery trying to find the rose garden. The children were enjoying themselves.

'How long are we going to be here?'

'Can we go fishing?'

'Don't pick up the flowers,' I said to my daughter.

'Can we have a séance thingy?'

'Don't be silly,' said my brother. 'You kids come here and try to find your Pop. Fifty cents for whoever finds him first.'

'Only fifty cents?' I said.

'All right, a dollar for whoever finds Grandad.'

During the next twenty minutes lots of grandads were found.

'Here he is!' said one of my nieces.

'Well no, he wasn't Italian and he wasn't a woman, so close but not close enough,' I said.

'That's a bit better, mate,' my brother said to my son. 'You've found a man. Good boy, but it's not your Pop. Let's just look a bit closer.'

'Don't pick the flowers, please,' I said to my daughter as she eyed a bouquet in an old glass jar.

We eventually found him; an old McDonald's wrapper was covering his plaque. There was a blank plaque next to his. Mum's.

It had started to drizzle. 'Hidden under a junk food packet in the rose garden,' my brother said. 'Dad would have wanted it this way.' We laughed and the kids soon joined in.

'Come on,' my brother said. 'It's a sign. Let's go to Macca's.'

'I found him, do I get my dollar?' I asked as we walked out through the graves.

'No, Bill, you don't,' Vaughan said.

'Leave those flowers alone, please,' I said as I held my daughter's hand.

Outside the departure gates my brother and I shook hands.

'Take care of yourself,' he said.

'You too.'

When you arch up into the air from Brisbane Airport you soar over Moreton Bay. I peered through the window down at the Redcliffe Peninsula. I always feel sad to see the old home from high in the sky; it means I'm leaving, and a part of me is moving further away from where I grew up.

Our lives go by, time passes and as Anne at the school reunion said, we drift away. But sometimes the tides of time bear us back and forth and there, floating in its stream, things can happen. If it is good and the tide is right, wonderful things happen. You just have to open your eyes and see them. For the next few weeks I didn't do that. I worked hard and hardly saw my family. I told myself when things quietened down I would spend more time with them.

But I did walk my son to school as often as I could; have done since he started. But lately something had changed. There was still the same early morning chaos – yelling at the dog, yelling for teeth to be cleaned, trying to find keys, trying to find wallet, yelling for teeth to be cleaned, yelling at my daughter that I didn't mean the dog's teeth. Coffee, breakfast, lunches packed. Out the door, on our way.

About a month ago, over dinner, my son asked me if my dad had ever walked me to school.

'Well, no,' I told him. 'Not once that I can remember. Got given the odd lift in the truck but no, he never walked me to school.'

I didn't think anything of it.

So here we were, on a regular school day; my son grabbed his lunch from his mum, opened the door. 'Come on, I'll take you up,' I said.

I was out the door when I heard him say quietly, 'Okay.'

We'd walked the route dozens of times. Soon as we stepped through the gate we could see it was going to be a beautiful, clear late winter's day.

'Nice day,' I said.

'It'll be a pearler, Dad,' my boy said in a broad accent. We laughed.

Next door our neighbour Rod stood at his mailbox cleaning out his junk mail. He waved. 'Hi, men. Anybody need carpet cleaning, or painted plates with Elvis on them or ... property investment advice?'

'Not today, thanks,' I said.

My son asked why people would want a plate with Elvis Presley on it. Rod provided the answer. 'People will buy just about anything, they just need a reason.' He waved his junk mail at the world. 'This is the reason.'

'They might like a plate because they like Elvis,' my boy said.

'They might ...' Rod paused, then said, 'He's done it again,' nodding to an old brown Falcon, stopped in the middle of the road.

It was Old Russ. He'd been stalling it a lot lately. We walked over to give him a push. The last time we tried to push it he'd left the handbrake on. My son asked Old Russ if he left it on this time. 'No,' he said. 'Car's a bit heavy. I'm getting fatter, too many Tim Tams.' We pushed the car and Old Russ sputtered away with a wave that only old men can give: a small, falling wave of the index finger. I thought of my father. He waved like that. My son laughed; he liked the way Old Russ waved. He asked me if Old Russ would like an Elvis plate. I said I didn't think so. We walked in silence for a while and then my son said that Old Russ's wife Lois used to give him bickies at the op shop. I nodded. My son was quiet for a moment and then he asked me how many people in the street had died since we had lived here. Lois had died just a month before.

'Quite a few,' I said. We passed the house of an old man who'd feed the parrots in summer and sing to them in Italian. He died two years ago. Then there was the old woman across the road who had died in her sleep. Asthma. The tall man with the ginger moustache who'd whistle while he walked and wave when he saw you and touch his hat and say, 'How do.' He died of cancer. There was 'the Pope', a man who bore an incredible resemblance to the recently departed Pope John Paul and who would ride about on an old pushbike wearing a never-ending series of different protective headgear. Sometimes it was a full-face motorbike helmet or a riding helmet or even an old cricket helmet complete with a crest and face grille. I hadn't seen him for months. Perhaps he had died and I hadn't noticed. 'Quite a few,' I repeated.

My son said he hoped I'd live to be at least a hundred and seventy-five. I smiled and ruffled his hair. I looked at him and I thought of the first time death had intruded upon my life. I would have been about the same age as my son. It was Jonsey the fireman. One night he'd gone fishing off the Woody Point jetty and somehow the car he was in had ended up in the sea. Jonsey with the laughing eyes and crinkled face, the kind growly voice and the happy whistle had died of a heart attack as he tried to free himself from the submerged vehicle. When Mum told me I wandered up the backyard and climbed the big Moreton Bay fig and stared down at the fire station. I tried to piece it all together but I couldn't. I cried without really knowing why and I knew that even though it'd still be fun living next door to the fire station, it'd never be quite the same again.

Before I could say anything more, Elaine appeared on the opposite side of the road. My son and I said, 'Hi, Elaine', she looked at us, then yelled, 'Oh yes, you can say that!' Then added, 'There's something *happening* with this day!'

Elaine would stalk the streets, wild-eyed and yelling, and waving bits of paper at people. She wasn't dangerous, but there had been a few complaints lately from some of the families who had recently moved into the area.

'Not many people talk to her now,' my son said, walking on ahead of me. 'If they did she mightn't yell so loud.'

I looked at my boy. 'Maybe.'

Something was happening with this day, but before I could figure out exactly what, a voice called from a car: 'Buongiorno, Guillermo! Buongiorno, Clemente!' It was Frank, the local Italian–Australian real estate agent. I waved, and my son yelled, 'Buongiorno, Frankie! Salute la Doggies!' Frank laughed and beeped his horn.

'You speak Italian?'

My son smiled. 'Learnt that at school.'

We crossed the busy street where Big Peter the Greek lolly-pop crossing man was blowing his whistle. He bellowed, 'Bewdiful day. He's gonna be big, your boy! He's growing!'

I nodded. We walked on and waved to Ivan in his barber shop, then passed 'Vic's Fruit and Veg'. My son laughed and told me how our dog Doug had a habit of cocking his leg on the old onions outside. He was always stopped before he could wee – but he kept trying. My son turned to me and said, 'You can never trust onions, Dad.'

When we neared the school, my son caught sight of one of his mates, Josh, and he told me that Josh walked by himself to school. This is when I understand, or think I do, that perhaps I'm in the way. Maybe my son wants to walk by himself too, with his friends. I feel a bit embarrassed. 'You know, mate, if you want to walk here, to school, by yourself, that's okay. You can, you know.'

He shrugs his shoulders the way ten-year-old boys do. 'Yeah, I know.'

I look at him, all arms and legs, bounding off, growing so fast. I remember holding him as a newborn at the hospital. Just staring at him. And holding him. Now someone's yelling to him and he catches a football one-handed, manages not to trip over his feet, and in a deft manoeuvre rockets back a kick. He stands with his mates.

I feel redundant. Something is happening with this day. Something. But as I turn to walk away I hear his voice. 'I love you, Dad!' His friends all laugh a bit. I think it came out louder than he intended but he keeps smiling and waves to me. I wave back. Perhaps he was just following the advice from my father of never being afraid to let the world know he was alive. Perhaps he was just being who he is.

Either way I knew Elaine was right: something is happening today. Life and change and love. Something wonderful. I walk off in no particular direction and look up into the blue sky and beyond and hear the words of an old song Dad would often hum:

Love is the sweetest thing
What else on earth could ever bring
Such happiness to everything
As loves old story

Love is the strangest thing
No song of birds upon the wing
Shall in our hearts more sweetly sing
Than loves old story

Whatever hearts may desire
Whatever fate may send
This is the tale that never will tire
This is the song without end

Love is the greatest thing
The oldest yet, the latest thing
I only hope that fate may bring
Loves story to you.

Acknowledgments

I'd like to acknowledge the following, in no particular order of importance. Peter Bolton, Rick MaCosker, Sarah Watt, Clem and Stella McInnes, Anna Reynolds, Bernadette 'Batman' Foley, Amy Hurrell, Vanessa Radnidge and all at Hachette Livre Australia.

Thank you.